Praise for EQ *Applied*

* * * * *

"*EQ Applied* is well researched, full of interesting stories, and a joy to read. It's a great asset to companies looking to gain insights into leadership and management and improve their corporate culture as a whole."

MARSHALL GOLDSMITH, world-renowned leadership thinker and bestselling author of *Triggers* and *What Got You Here Won't Get You There*

"What is emotional intelligence, really? In *EQ Applied,* Justin Bariso answers that question completely. With a fresh perspective, he shows us a different side to emotional intelligence—and then teaches readers how to grow their own, step by step. This is a must read."

REBECCA JARVIS, Emmy Award–winning journalist and host of the *No Limits with Rebecca Jarvis* podcast

"A captivating read that takes much of what we've learned about emotional behavior and shows you how to put those lessons to work."

DR. HENDRIE WEISINGER, Ph.D., *New York Times* bestselling author of *Performing Under Pressure*

"Most books about emotional intelligence aren't written with a lot of emotional intelligence. In *EQ Applied*, however, Justin Bariso has stopped to think about how you learn, how you feel, and how you prefer to be talked to. You'll learn even more than you thought you did."

CHRIS MATYSZCZYK, president of Howard Raucous LLC and creator of CNET's *Technically Incorrect* and Inc.'s *Absurdly Driven* columns

"From getting more out of the feedback I receive, to figuring out how I can be more persuasive in a positive way, to how I can better harness my emotions, I got so many real-world lessons out of *EQ Applied* and I'm sure you'll feel the same. It's the practical approach to emotional intelligence we've all been waiting for."

JEREMY GOLDMAN, founder of the Firebrand Group and author of *Going Social* and *Getting to Like*

"In *EQ Applied*, Justin Bariso reveals a fascinating look at why in this day and age, emotional intelligence is more important than ever. His concepts around behavior will help you interpret other people—and yourself."

SALLY HOGSHEAD, *New York Times* bestselling author of *Fascinate* and *How the World Sees You*

"Understanding the role of emotions in the workplace and dealing intelligently with them is the key to business success. This amazing book explains why—and exactly how to do it."

ALEXANDER KJERULF, Chief Happiness Officer, Woohoo Inc.

EQ APPLIED

HOW TO MAKE **EMOTIONS** WORK **FOR** YOU, INSTEAD OF AGAINST **YOU**

APPLIED

THE REAL-WORLD GUIDE TO EMOTIONAL INTELLIGENCE

JUSTIN BARISO

BOROUGH HALL

BOROUGH HALL
Germany

ISBN 978-3-9819841-2-5 (Hardcover)
ISBN 978-3-9819841-1-8 (Paperback)
ISBN 978-3-9819841-0-1 (eBook)

This book is not intended as a substitute for the medical
advice of physicians. The reader should regularly
consult a physician in matters relating to his/her health
and particularly with respect to any symptoms that
may require diagnosis or medical attention.

In some instances names and identifying
characteristics have been changed to protect
the privacy of the individuals involved.

Produced by Page Two
www.pagetwostrategies.com
Cover design by Aksara Mantra
Interior design by Taysia Louie

18 19 20 21 22 5 4 3 2 1

www.eqapplied.com

*For Dominika, Jonah, and Lily, who have taught
me more than could fill a million books*

Contents

Introduction 1

1 **From Theory to Practice:** What
Real-World Emotional Intelligence Looks Like 5

2 **Under Control:** Training and
Honing Your Emotional Abilities 17

3 **Creatures of Habit:** How Thoughts
and Habits Affect Your Emotions 37

4 **Diamonds in the Rough:** Why You
Should Treat All Feedback as a Gift 53

5 **The Truth about Empathy:** The Good,
the Bad, and the Misunderstood 69

6 **The Power of Influence:** How
Emotional Connection Breaks Down
Barriers and Changes Minds 91

7 **Building Bridges:** Cultivating Deeper,
Healthier, More Loyal Relationships 109

8 **The Dark Side:** From Dr. Jekyll to Mr. Hyde 131

9 **Moving Forward:** Embracing
the Emotional Journey 153

Appendix: The Ten Commandments
of Emotional Intelligence 159
Acknowledgments 163
References 169
Bibliography 181
About the Author 191
Contact and Speaking 193

Introduction

IN 1995, PSYCHOLOGIST and science journalist Daniel Goleman published a book introducing most of the world to the nascent concept of emotional intelligence. The idea—that our ability to understand and manage emotions greatly increases our chances of success—quickly took off, and it went on to greatly influence the way people think about emotions and human behavior.

In the twenty-plus years since Goleman's book burst onto the scene, the world has changed dramatically, and the need for emotional intelligence has only intensified.

Consider that a fractured political climate is now the norm, with candidates using emotions like fear and anger as "weapons of mass persuasion." Passionate followers—quick to judge the "other" as stupid or incorrigible—pursue heated discourse and hurl ad hominem attacks, making calm and rational discussion all but impossible.

War, globalization, and increasing urbanization continue to push people of different races, cultures, and backgrounds into closer proximity. Rich and poor become neighbors in overpopulated cities. In some countries, refugee camps have sprung up in firmly established neighborhoods. But unfamiliarity breeds fear, and these differences fuel suspicion and worry.

The internet has put an immense amount of information at our fingertips. But as news travels at lightning speed, it's more difficult than ever to tell fact from fiction. The result? An era of post-truth, where appeals to emotion and personal belief have become more influential than objective facts.

The proliferation of smartphones and mobile devices has replaced brief moments of observation and self-reflection with constant reading and responding to messages, checking of social media feeds, or simply browsing the internet—actions spurred on by feelings of anxiety, boredom, and fear of missing out. The ability to communicate with practically anyone, at any time, inspires us to overshare in an emotional moment, revealing sensitive information we later regret.

As this Pavlovian addiction to our devices destroys our self-control, it simultaneously diminishes our ability to think for ourselves. The websites we frequent play a major role in shaping our emotions; the stories we read, the news we consume, the videos we watch all shape our moods and thoughts, slowly molding our opinions and ideologies—without us even realizing it.

Consider also that as the world has evolved, so has our understanding of emotional intelligence.

When the term was first proposed, many considered emotional intelligence inherently virtuous. Proponents touted it as the end-all solution to various problems, from bullying at school to weak employee engagement. But it's become evident that, like traditional intelligence, this tool can be used for both ethical and unethical purposes. For example, researchers have demonstrated how some people with high emotional intelligence use their skills to selfishly influence or manipulate others.

But building your own emotional intelligence can help you identify and combat these attempts. By increasing your knowledge about emotions and how they work, you'll be able to better understand yourself—and the reasons behind the decisions you make. This will enable you to devise strategies that will proactively shape your emotional reactions, to avoid saying and doing things you will later regret, and to motivate yourself to act when necessary. Eventually, you'll learn to use emotions to help others as well, creating deeper and more meaningful relationships in the process.

These are just some of the reasons why we need emotional intelligence today more than ever.

To guide us into the topic, we'll explore the following questions:

· How can you transform your strongest emotions from a destructive force to a power for good?
· How can asking the right questions and expanding your emotional vocabulary help you become more self-aware?
· Why is it so difficult to cultivate self-control? How can you improve your ability to do so?
· How can knowledge about the brain and the way it works help you shape your emotional habits?
· How can you get the most from the feedback you receive, whether positive or negative?
· How can you deliver feedback in a way that benefits others?
· How can empathy help you, and how can it hurt you?
· How can you be more persuasive or influence others in a positive way?
· How can emotional intelligence help you cultivate—and maintain—deeper, more meaningful relationships?
· How can you protect yourself from the people who use the principles of persuasion and influence to harm or manipulate you or others?

I'll use a combination of fascinating research and real-life stories to provide practical answers to these questions. I'll also get personal, explaining how emotional intelligence taught me to lead, and also how it taught me to follow. I'll relate how the ability to understand and reach others emotionally helped me to woo my wife and made me a better husband and father. But I'll also detail the dangers I encountered along the way and show why working to increase and apply your emotional intelligence quotient—your EQ—is only one piece of the puzzle to becoming the best version of yourself.

The final goal is simple: I want to help you make emotions work for you, instead of against you.

1

From Theory to Practice

What Real-World Emotional Intelligence Looks Like

• • • • •

*The emotions of man are stirred more
quickly than man's intelligence.*

OSCAR WILDE

IN 1997, STEVE Jobs returned to Apple, the company he
cofounded, and proceeded to lead one of the most remarkable turnarounds in history. As CEO, he brought Apple
back from the brink of bankruptcy, aiding its transformation
into the most valuable company on the planet.

All of this success is even more impressive when we consider that, just twelve years earlier, Jobs was forced out of the
company he helped build.

Jobs had a reputation as brilliant and inspiring—but he
was also known to be overbearing, impatient, and petulant.

Circumstances had eventually become so difficult between him and Apple's board of directors that the group stripped him of major responsibilities and rendered him nearly powerless. Jobs, feeling betrayed, left the company and founded a new start-up named NeXT.

Notably, a number of high-ranking Apple employees followed their former boss to his new company. At the time, Jobs was a cocky, thirty-one-year-old multimillionaire who was almost always convinced he was right. He was harsh and demanding, and he could be very demeaning. So why would this group of sharp, focused individuals leave secure positions to continue working with him?

Andy Cunningham gives us a hint. As Jobs's PR agent, she helped launch the Macintosh and continued to work with Jobs at NeXT and Pixar. I spoke to Cunningham to understand what she treasured about working with her famous former boss.

"I spent five years working closely with Steve and it was phenomenal," Cunningham told me. "What people on the outside saw—the inspiring interviews and brilliant keynotes—that was who he was. And while he could also be very harsh, it was an honor to work with him. The great things in life involve sacrifice, but the tradeoff makes it all worth it.

"Steve touched me emotionally every day with amazement, anger, and satisfaction all at once. He took me way beyond where I ever thought I would go."

If you ever saw Jobs deliver one of his famous product launches, you witnessed this ability in action. Jobs knew how to tap into the sentiments of his audience. Consumers wanted Apple devices because of the way those products made them *feel*.

Critics, though, argue that whatever success Jobs achieved was *despite* his inability to deal well with emotions—both his and those of others.

So, was Steve Jobs emotionally intelligent?

Before answering that question, we need to understand the core concept of emotional intelligence.

Defining emotional intelligence

When Daniel Goleman published *Emotional Intelligence* in 1995, few had heard of the term. In academic circles, it was a new concept—a theory formed by two psychologists, John D. Mayer and Peter Salovey, which posited that just as people have a wide range of intellectual abilities, they also have a wide range of emotional skills that profoundly affect their thinking and actions.

But that all changed once *TIME* magazine featured the idea as its cover story on October 2, 1995. In bold, striking fashion, the magazine asked:

"What's your EQ?"

Emotional Intelligence would spend a year and a half on the *New York Times* bestseller list and eventually be translated into forty languages. The *Harvard Business Review* described the concept as "revolutionary" and "paradigm-shattering." This sudden popularity caused many to rethink their views on intellect and emotional behavior.

But while the term "emotional intelligence" was new at the time, the concept behind it really wasn't.

For centuries, leaders and philosophers have advised their followers to consider how emotions affect behavior. And in the early 1980s, distinguished psychologist Howard Gardner theorized that rather than intelligence consisting of a single general ability, there are several types of "intelligences" at which an individual may excel—including the ability to understand one's own feelings and the role those feelings play in behavior (intrapersonal intelligence), as well as the ability to understand emotional behavior in others (interpersonal intelligence).

Nonetheless, Goleman, Mayer, Salovey, and others helped us look at emotions more closely. As the field of emotional intelligence grew, it led to further study and research and brought new insights to light.

So, how do we define emotional intelligence? In their original article, Mayer and Salovey described it this way:

> Emotional intelligence is the ability to monitor one's own and others' feelings and emotions, to discriminate among them and to use this information to guide one's thinking and actions.

Notice that emotional intelligence, by definition, emphasizes practical use. It's not just knowledge about emotions and how they work; it's an individual's ability to apply that knowledge to manage their own behavior or relationships with others, to attain a desired result.

Put simply: emotional intelligence is the ability to make emotions work for you, instead of against you.

What does that look like in real life?

Let's say you're involved in a conversation that suddenly turns from friendly disagreement to passionate argument. As you recognize the situation has become emotionally charged, you work to get your feelings "under control." You may even take leave to prevent yourself from saying or doing something you'll later regret.

Or, you may recognize that your conversation partner is speaking and acting irrationally, due to being in an emotional state, even as you remain calm. You then make efforts to defuse the situation, perhaps by gently changing the subject. If it's necessary to continue the discussion, you may decide to wait until the person is in a calmer state of mind, while giving careful thought to how you could broach the subject in the best way.

The point of these examples isn't that you should avoid any type of conflict or passionate discussion. Rather, it means learning to identify when they're coming so you're not walking into them inadvertently and dealing with them in a way that you later regret. Emotional intelligence also involves learning to see your thoughts and feelings from the perspective of others, so that your emotions don't prevent them from discounting your opinion before they've even heard it.

But we've only begun to scratch the surface.

Emotional intelligence is the ability to make emotions work for you, instead of against you.

The four abilities

To understand the full scope of emotional intelligence, it's helpful to break it down into four general abilities.*

Self-awareness is the ability to identify and understand your own emotions and how they affect you. This means

---

* The "four-ability" framework used in this book is my interpretation of emotional intelligence, based on Goleman's model that includes four "domains," which he describes as self-awareness, self-management, social awareness, and relationship management.

recognizing how emotions impact your thoughts and actions (and vice versa) and how your feelings can help or hinder you from achieving your goals.

Self-awareness includes the ability to recognize your emotional tendencies, strengths, and weaknesses.

Self-management is the ability to manage emotions in a way that allows you to accomplish a task, reach a goal, or provide a benefit. It includes the quality of self-control, which is the ability to control your emotional reactions.

Since emotions involve your natural, instinctive feelings and are influenced by your unique brain chemistry, you can't always control how you feel. But you can control the way you act (or refrain from acting) upon those feelings. Practicing self-control can therefore reduce the chance you say or do something you later regret, especially in an emotionally charged situation.

Over a longer period of time, self-management can even help you proactively shape your emotional tendencies.

Social awareness is the ability to accurately perceive the feelings of others and understand how those feelings influence behavior.

Social awareness is founded on the quality of empathy, which allows you to see and feel things from the perspective of others. Empathy keeps you in tune with others' wants and needs, and it equips you to better satisfy those desires, increasing the value you have to offer. Social awareness also provides you with a more complete picture of others and helps you understand the role emotions play in your relationships.

Relationship management is the ability to get the most out of your connections with others.

It includes the ability to influence through your communication and behavior. Instead of trying to force others into action, you use insight and persuasion to motivate them to act on their own accord.

Relationship management also involves bringing emotional benefits to others. Doing so gradually increases the level of trust and strengthens the bond between you and your partners.

Each of the four abilities is interconnected and naturally complements the others; however, one isn't always *dependent* on another. You will naturally excel at certain aspects of the four abilities and display weaknesses in others. For example, you may be great at perceiving your own emotions, yet you struggle to manage those feelings. The key to strengthening your emotional intelligence is first to identify your personal traits and tendencies and then to develop strategies to maximize your strengths and minimize your weaknesses.

Consider the trait of social awareness. The ability to anticipate and understand the feelings of others can help you avoid creating unnecessary offense, a skill that makes you more likable and draws others to you. But that same attribute can become a weakness if it inhibits your ability to speak up when you should or stops you from giving critical (yet helpful) feedback for fear of how others will react.

High social awareness is therefore most effective when it is tempered with the other three abilities. Self-awareness helps you identify when this perception of others' feelings is holding you back from saying or doing something that could be helpful. Self-management involves preparing yourself for such situations and cultivating the habits that motivate you to action. Finally, the ability to manage relationships will help you say whatever you need to say in a way that accomplishes your purpose while increasing influence, mitigating hurt feelings, and building trust.

As you continue reading, you'll learn the different aspects of each of the four skills of emotional intelligence and how they apply to you personally.

What is EQ? Can it be measured?

Despite many researchers' preference to abbreviate emotional intelligence as EI in studies and academic journals, the term EQ (shorthand for "emotional intelligence quotient") has become popular and easily recognizable in multiple languages.

This makes sense, if you think about how we use IQ in daily conversation. In sports, we refer to those who have a superior understanding of the game as having a high IQ ("they have a high basketball or football IQ"), meaning they understand the rules and strategy of the game. This ability isn't really something that's measured, but it's practical and easy to understand.

In a similar way, when we speak about a person's EQ, we mean their ability to understand emotions and how they work. But the value of that knowledge is limited if it can't be put to use.

In other words, true emotional intelligence = EQ, applied.

There are numerous assessments that claim to measure emotional intelligence. But tests like these have limited value: they may give you an idea as to how much you know about emotions and their effect on behavior, but they can't evaluate your ability to put that knowledge to work in everyday situations.

Rather than trying to quantify your emotional intelligence, it's more productive to focus on developing a growth mindset.*

Begin by asking yourself: In what situations do I find that emotions work against me?

---

* The concept of the growth mindset has gained popularity in recent years, partially due to the work of Stanford psychology professor Carol Dweck. In her book *Mindset*, Dweck advocates that individuals who believe their talents can be developed through hard work, good strategies, and input from others (growth mindset) tend to achieve more than those who believe their talents are innate gifts with finite development potential (fixed mindset). We'll further explore the connection of the growth mindset to emotional intelligence in chapter three.

For example:

- Your temper caused you to say or do something you later regretted.
- You agreed to a request because you were in a good mood, only to later realize that you didn't really think things through.
- Your inability to understand someone's feelings caused anxiety or led to a breakdown in communication.
- You found it difficult to manage conflict.
- You missed out on a great opportunity because of undue anxiety or fear.

Once you've identified a few areas, move on to step two: ask someone you trust to give you feedback. It could be your spouse or another family member, a close friend, a mentor, or another confidant. Be clear that you're working to improve yourself and you need them to honestly answer the question: In what situations have you seen emotions working against me? Allow enough time so that they can give the question some thought, then discuss their answer.

This practice is valuable because your perspective is primarily formed subconsciously and is influenced by a myriad of factors, including the following:

- Where you grew up
- How you were raised
- Who you associate with
- What you choose to think about

The goal in this discussion is not to determine whether others' views about you are right or wrong. Rather, you want to learn the differences between how they view you compared to how you view yourself, along with the consequences of those differences. Seriously considering this question, along with any honest feedback you receive, helps you build self-awareness and identify points of weakness that you consider a priority.

The ultimate goal

Getting back to the question in our intro: Was Steve Jobs emotionally intelligent?

He certainly found a way to motivate and inspire many of those he worked with, along with millions of consumers around the globe—even across language and cultural barriers. These are all signs of exceptional social awareness, as well as the ability to influence, which is a key aspect of relationship management.

But what about Jobs's communication style, which angered and frustrated many? He had become known for wild emotional swings and was perceived as arrogant and narcissistic. His manner pained many—including his family and others with whom he was close. Jobs himself blamed this on a lack of self-control. When his biographer Walter Isaacson asked him why he was sometimes so mean, Jobs replied: "This is who I am, and you can't expect me to be someone I'm not."

But Isaacson, who spent a significant amount of time with Jobs over the course of two years, and who interviewed more than a hundred of the famous entrepreneur's friends, relatives, competitors, and colleagues, believed differently.

"When he hurt people, it was not because he was lacking in emotional awareness," writes Isaacson. "Quite the contrary: he could size people up, understand their inner thoughts, and know how to relate to them, cajole them, or hurt them at will."

Would Jobs have changed a few things if he could go back and do it again? It's impossible to say. But in his story lies a vital lesson: emotional intelligence manifests itself in various ways. In addition to deciding *which* abilities you wish to develop, you must also choose *how* you're going to use them.

It's important to realize that just as "traditionally" intelligent people have different personality types, so do those who possess high emotional intelligence. Direct or subtle, extroverted or introverted, naturally empathetic or not—none of these factors determines your EQ.

Developing your emotional acumen is about identifying your natural abilities, tendencies, strengths, and weaknesses. It means learning to understand, manage, and maximize all of those traits so you can accurately perceive how your emotions affect your thoughts, words, and actions (and vice versa), and how those words and actions affect others.

Instead of attempting to simply raise your EQ, my goal is to provide you with the strategies you need to put your EQ to work—to reach your goals, to cultivate a mindset of continuous growth, and to use your knowledge in a way you and others can be proud of.

That's EQ, applied: making emotions work for you, instead of against you.

2

Under Control

Training and Honing Your Emotional Abilities

• • • • •

Your emotions are the slaves to your thoughts,
and you are the slave to your emotions.

ELIZABETH GILBERT

O N JANUARY 15, 2009, US Airways Flight 1549 began
its route from New York City to Charlotte, North Caro-
lina. For Captain Chesley B. "Sully" Sullenberger III,
it was just another routine flight, one of thousands he had
flown over a career that spanned decades.

But just before the plane had risen to three thousand feet,
Sullenberger and his first officer Jeff Skiles noticed a flock of
geese flying directly at them. In less than a second, the birds
collided with the airplane, severely damaging both engines.

"As the birds hit the plane, it felt like we were being pelted
by heavy rain or hail," says Sullenberger. "It sounded like

the worst thunderstorm I'd ever heard... Realizing that we were without engines, I knew that this was the worst aviation challenge I'd ever faced. It was the most sickening, pit-of-your-stomach, falling-through-the-floor feeling I had ever experienced."

Sullenberger experienced a rush of thoughts, beginning with two that were rooted in disbelief: *This can't be happening. This doesn't happen to me.*

Those thoughts were accompanied by what the pilot describes as a rush of adrenaline and a spike in blood pressure. In the following minutes, he and Skiles would need to make a series of quick decisions. There were countless factors to be weighed, with no time for extensive communication or detailed calculation. Emergency procedures that were designed to take minutes needed to be performed in seconds.

Drawing on years of experience, Sullenberger decided that his best chance of saving the 155 lives on board was to attempt something he had never done before; in fact, hardly any pilots had been trained to perform such a feat. Sullenberger would attempt to land in the Hudson River.

Against all odds, just 208 seconds after the engines were struck, Sullenberger valiantly and safely guided the plane into the river, near midtown Manhattan. And due to the collective efforts of the captain, the first officer, traffic control, the flight attendants, and dozens of first responders, all 155 passengers and crew survived. The event has become known as the Miracle on the Hudson.

Looking back, Sullenberger remembers what he felt as if it had just happened.

"I was aware of my body," he explains. "I could feel an adrenaline rush. I'm sure that my blood pressure and pulse spiked. But I also knew I had to concentrate on the tasks at hand and not let the sensations in my body distract me."

For millions around the world, what Sullenberger accomplished on that winter day was superhuman, an amazing act of heroism. How did the captain, along with the first officer and traffic control officer, manage to keep his emotions in control and pull off this "miracle"?

The answers are found not in those amazing moments, but rather in the years of training, practice, and experience that preceded them.

Years of preparation

Sullenberger's success in those incredible moments was no coincidence. A quick look at his resume gives an indication as to the skills he had collected over the years: flying fighter jets as a former Air Force pilot, flying commercial aircrafts for nearly thirty years, investigating accidents, and instructing flight crews on how to respond to crises in the air.

"I think in many ways, as it turned out, my entire life up to that moment had been a preparation to handle that particular moment," Sullenberger told journalist Katie Couric in an interview.

The Miracle on the Hudson well illustrates the power of the first two abilities of emotional intelligence: self-awareness and self-management. In that harrowing moment, Sullenberger managed to demonstrate remarkable self-awareness: the ability to acknowledge and understand the emotional and physical reaction his body was experiencing. He then exercised amazing self-control (a key facet of self-management), as he imposed his will on the situation.

Couric asked Sullenberger if this was a hard thing to do—namely, to overcome such a strong physiological reaction and enforce calm on the situation. Sullenberger's reply was somewhat surprising: "No. It just took some concentration."

While you may never encounter circumstances quite like this, you *will* be faced with life-altering situations. Your ability to demonstrate self-awareness and self-management will impact the decisions you make in these moments. But what can you do to develop those abilities?

It all begins with preparation.

That's the purpose of this chapter: to introduce you to the tools and methods that will help you build self-awareness and practice self-management. I'll demonstrate how asking the right questions and expanding your emotional vocabulary can help you learn more about yourself, and I'll show you how to use that knowledge to your advantage. Then, I'll explain the importance of focusing on your thoughts in emotional moments and share a practical mnemonic device to help you do so.

Ask and reflect

Emotional intelligence begins with self-awareness. We often go through life reacting, never taking the time to think about how or why we respond the way we do. This method of operation limits the control we have over our actions and tendencies.

One of the best ways to develop self-awareness is to ask the right questions. Doing so can broaden your perspective and help you see yourself through the eyes of others. Additionally, you'll gain insight into their thinking and feeling processes.

As discussed in the previous chapter, you can learn a lot about yourself by asking a single question: In what situations do I find that emotions work against me? Here are some other questions you can ask:

- How would I (or you) describe my communication style? Am I direct? Brash? Clear? Ambiguous? Subtle? Tactful? How would others describe my communication style?

- What effect does my communication have on others?
- How would I (or you) describe the way I make decisions? Do I tend to make decisions slowly or quickly? What factors influence me?
- How does my current mood affect my thoughts and decision-making?
- How would I (or you) rate my self-esteem and self-confidence? How do my self-esteem and self-confidence affect my decision-making?
- What are my emotional strengths? What are my emotional weaknesses?
- Am I open to other perspectives? Am I too easily swayed by others?
- Should I be more or less skeptical? Why?
- Do I tend to focus on the positive or negative traits of others?
- What traits in others bother me? Why?
- Do I generally give others the benefit of the doubt? Why or why not?
- Do I find it difficult to admit when I'm wrong? Why or why not?

This is just a small sample; the goal is not to sit down and comprehensively answer all of these questions in one day. Rather, it's to cultivate a learning mindset. Asking yourself these questions will inspire you to ask more questions, leading to greater learnings about yourself and how emotions influence you.

> **TRY THIS:** Carve out some time this week to answer a few of the above questions. Avoid superficial responses. Think deeply and search yourself thoroughly, allowing at least five minutes with each question. (It helps to write your answers down, rather than just thinking them.) Try to brainstorm more

questions you'd like to answer about your feelings. Then, the next time you experience a strong emotional reaction, ask yourself why you acted the way you did and what else you can learn from the experience.

Use your emotional vocabulary

One day, you wake up with an intense pain that you've never felt before, so you decide to go to the doctor for help. Early into your visit, the doctor asks you to describe the pain you're feeling. Depending on your experience, you may use any of the following words: sharp, dull, burning, shooting, aching, cramping, gnawing, heavy, splitting, stabbing, nauseating, throbbing, tender. The more specific you can get in describing your pain, the easier it will be for your doctor to diagnose the problem and prescribe proper treatment.

It works similarly with your emotions: by using specific words to describe your feelings, you can better "diagnose" them—helping you understand where they're coming from, and why. The right words can help you get to the root cause of your feelings and better enable you to communicate them in a way others can understand.

To illustrate, let's say that you come home from a long day at work and get into an argument with your significant other. They ask you why you're in such a bad mood, and you're not sure. You could say that you're angry or upset, but after giving some thought to your feelings, you describe yourself as hurt or betrayed. The reason? A cutting remark your partner made that morning. You didn't say anything at the time because you thought you'd get over it, but now it's obvious that the wound is deeper than you realized. An honest conversation may help your partner understand how deeply their words affected you or better understand your feelings about a particular situation.

➤ **TRY THIS:** The next time you experience a strong emotional reaction, take time afterwards to process not only what you're feeling, but why. Try to put your feelings into words—the more specific the better. Then, determine what you want to do about the situation.

Focus on controlling your thoughts

Our emotions have tremendous impact on our behavior. That's why self-management, the ability to manage your feelings and control your reactions, is so important.

If you're better able to control your impulses, you can bring your actions into greater harmony with your values. This helps you develop qualities like determination and endurance, which will increase your effectiveness in reaching goals. And self-management isn't only about preventing regrettable action; it also means finding a way to spur or motivate yourself to step up and take action when doing so isn't easy.

So, how do you develop the control needed to make emotions work for you, instead of against you?

Since most of the emotions you experience occur almost instinctively, you can't control how you feel in any given moment. But you can control how you *react* to those feelings—by focusing on your thoughts.

This doesn't mean you can restrict thoughts from entering your mind. We've all had thoughts that we aren't proud of, and we can be greatly influenced by various factors beyond our control, including genetics and the environment in which we were raised.

But as it's been said: you may not be able to stop a bird from landing on your head, but you can keep it from building a nest.

Self-awareness and self-management go hand in hand. Once you've built a certain amount of self-awareness, you'll usually notice when your emotions are beginning to spiral out of control. We could compare your ability to direct your thoughts in these situations to a set of controls on your favorite media player. Just as these controls come in handy when watching a film or listening to music, the following methods are useful to help manage your emotional reactions.

1. Pause.

The pause is the most important of all the emotional tools in your toolbox. To pause, you must take time to stop and think before you speak or act. Doing so can prevent you from saying or doing something you'll later regret.

But the pause isn't only effective when dealing with upsetting situations. Often, we're tempted to jump on opportunities that look really good at the time but that we haven't really thought through. Have you ever found when shopping that you tend to overspend when in a good mood (or maybe a bad mood)? Use the pause to help you identify that mood and determine if you really want to make that purchase or if you're going to regret it later on.

There are various ways to use the pause, and you can practice it differently depending on the circumstances. When upset, you may find it helpful to count silently from one to ten. On other occasions, you may need to physically remove yourself from a situation.

The pause is easy in theory, difficult in practice. Even if you've developed good self-management skills, factors like added stress or a bad day can inhibit your ability to pause at any given time. That's why it's important to train yourself to use the pause regularly. In time, you'll create a habit of thoughtful reaction.

➤ **TRY THIS:** If you feel yourself beginning to respond emotionally to a situation, take a pause. If possible, go for a short walk. Once you've had the chance to calm down, come back and decide how you want to move forward.

2. Volume.

When you communicate, your conversation partner will often react in the same style or tone you choose. If you speak in a calm, rational voice, they'll respond similarly. Yell or scream, and they start yelling and screaming, too.

Here is where your volume control comes in: if you need to have an emotionally charged conversation, speak in a way that's calm and collected.

➤ **TRY THIS:** If the discussion begins to escalate, focus your efforts on "dialing it back" by softening your tone or even lowering your voice. You'll be surprised at how your partner follows your lead.

3. Mute.

If an interaction with another person turns emotional, and leaving the situation is not an option, you may need to hit the mute button. In other words, stop speaking.

This method is useful because at such a moment in time, sharing your point of view isn't going to help the situation; in contrast, it usually makes matters worse. By hitting the mute button, you allow the other person to express their feelings without interruption.

Of course, it's not easy to sit there and simply soak up another person's rant or tirade. How do you manage your own emotions in those moments?

> **TRY THIS:** Take a deep breath and remind yourself that both your mood and that of your communication partner are temporary. Remember that much of what they say at this point may be extreme or exaggerated; resist the urge to respond in kind.

In many cases, once the person has let everything out they'll calm down. As you remain on mute, be sure to...

4. Record.
Recording is concentrated listening, with the intent to learn more about the other person's perspective. In other words, don't listen to help figure out how to reply; instead, listen to understand.

> **TRY THIS:** As you tune into the other person, resist the urge to judge, offer advice, or even try to identify underlying problems and solutions.

Instead, focus on gathering information. The goal is to gain insight: to learn more about how the other person sees you, how they see themselves, and how they see the situation. Through attentive listening, you may identify gaps in your knowledge or perception, or discover basic misunderstandings you didn't know existed.

5. Rewind.
Emotionally charged discussions are often rooted in deep-seated issues. If left alone, these problems are likely to continue springing up. That's why you shouldn't take a pause or hit mute with the intent of completely forgetting the situation.

Instead, use rewind to revisit the topic at a later time, once all parties have had time to cool down.

➤ **TRY THIS:** Before revisiting a touchy topic, give careful thought as to where and when to speak, with the goal of calm and rational discussion.

It's also important to consider how you will reintroduce the subject. For example, opening with an apology, with an expression of gratitude, or by acknowledging where you and your communication partner agree may lead the other person to lower their guard and become more open to what you have to say.

6. Fast-forward.

Fast-forwarding to the end may ruin a film, but it's an extremely helpful skill when dealing with our emotions. If you find yourself in an emotionally charged moment, step back and think forward to the consequences of your actions—both short- and long-term.

For example, imagine a colleague has been showing romantic interest in you for years, despite your clear expressions that you're in a happy relationship and not interested. But one day, after a big fight with your partner, you think differently. Those advances are suddenly flattering—and tempting.

Now's the time to fast-forward. Forget about how you feel in the moment. Ask yourself: How will this decision affect you in a month? A year? Five years? Think about the effects your actions will have on your spouse, your family members, your conscience, and even your work.

➤ **TRY THIS:** If emotion is clouding your judgment, take a moment to fast-forward. Doing so can help you achieve clarity of mind and make sound decisions that you're proud of.

7. Trailer.

The trailer is useful when trying to get motivated or fight the tendency to procrastinate. While you may not be motivated to dedicate ninety minutes or more to watching a film you know nothing about, you're probably willing to watch a short trailer. Similarly, a five-minute trailer (or preview) of a task can convince your mind that it's worth it to follow through.

The trailer is another name for an old cognitive behavioral therapy trick known as "the five-minute rule." Here's how it works: force yourself to work on a task for just five minutes, with the understanding that you can quit after five minutes if you wish. Of course, more often than not, you'll be motivated to keep going. The trailer works because getting started on a major task is often the hardest part.

"We're scared of the big, amorphous blob of a task precisely because it *is* so big and ill-defined, and because we worry that it will take two hours or two days to get to the bottom of it," explains psychologist Andrea Bonoir. But conquering the psychological barriers of getting started gets your energy and momentum flowing—and makes you more likely to come back to the task and continue.

> **TRY THIS:** If you're struggling to find motivation to start a task, give it just five minutes.

The three-second trick that can save your relationships

We've seen how asking good questions can help build self-awareness and how pressing pause can lead to wiser decisions. Now, let's combine those two methods to see how asking yourself the right question, at the right moment, can help you effectively manage an emotional reaction.

For years I struggled with the tendency to speak too quickly, without thinking things through. To help mitigate this weakness, I began using a three-question method that I discovered through an unlikely source. Years ago, comedian Craig Ferguson gave the following advice in an interview:

There are three things you must always ask yourself before you say anything:

- Does this need to be said?
- Does this need to be said by me?
- Does this need to be said by me now?

With enough practice, it only takes a few seconds to go through these questions mentally. (Ferguson quipped that it took him three marriages to learn that lesson.)

For me, this quick mental dialogue is a lifesaver. It's helped me on more than one occasion to avoid saying something I'd quickly regret—both at home and in the workplace. It also doesn't discourage me from speaking up when appropriate; there are times when the answer to all three questions is a resounding yes—even when what I need to say isn't comfortable for me or the recipient. When those times come, this method allows me to speak with confidence and to be assertive when it counts.

But maybe your tendency is the opposite. If you naturally hesitate to voice your opinion, the last thing you want to do is discourage yourself from speaking up. Instead, you may use the following question to help manage your emotional response: If I don't say this now, will I regret it later?

These are just two examples. The key is to first use questions and reflection to get to know your habits and tendencies. Once you build this type of self-awareness, you can brainstorm your own questions, with the goal of keeping your emotions balanced.

➤ **TRY THIS:** Take some time to ponder your personal communication style. Do you tend to put your foot in your mouth, agree too quickly to commitments, or otherwise say something you later regret? Or do you tend to stay silent, later wishing you had expressed yourself?

Try using the questions on the previous page (or brainstorm a few of your own) to help you effectively manage your emotions, and then act accordingly.

Never make a permanent decision based on a temporary emotion.

Managing moods

Anger, frustration, fear, envy, sadness, disgust—we all have negative emotions, and they can certainly prove harmful if left unchecked.

At times, these feelings may be indicative of a physical problem. Are you hungry? Low blood sugar can suddenly put you in the worst of moods, but a quick snack can help bring you back to normal. Are you sleeping enough? Research indicates that lack of proper sleep can severely hamper your ability to manage your emotional reactions.

At times, negative emotion can be useful—if you learn to harness them effectively. Here are two ways to do this.

1. Use negative emotions as a catalyst for change.

In her book *Emotional Agility*, Harvard psychologist Susan David explains how such feelings actually encourage us to slow down and think, to pay more attention to subtle details instead of relying on quick conclusions.

"'Negative' moods summon a more attentive, accommodating thinking style that leads you to really examine facts in a fresh and creative way," writes David. "When we're overly cheerful, we tend to neglect important threats and dangers... It's when we're in a bit of a funk that we focus and dig down. People in negative moods tend to be less gullible and more skeptical, while happy folks may accept easy answers and trust false smiles."

To derive benefit from negative emotions, you need to decide what you're going to do with them.

For example, David relates how she began traveling around the world to meet clients for her coaching consultancy. As she sat in a posh hotel room observing the beautiful view and enjoying room service, she experienced a feeling she didn't expect—guilt. She couldn't help but dwell on the fact that while she was enjoying her freedom, her husband was alone with the children.

"I have realized that my guilt can help me set my priorities and sometimes realign my actions," she writes. "My on-the-road guilt signals to me that I miss my children and value my family. It reminds me that my life is heading in the right direction when I'm spending more time with them. My guilt is a flashing arrow pointing toward the people I love and the life I want to lead."

2. Use negative emotions to achieve heightened focus.

To do this, you must find a way to recategorize your feelings, channeling them into positive action.

Lisa Feldman Barrett, a neuroscientist and professor of psychology at Northeastern University, explains one way you can do this in her book, *How Emotions Are Made*. If you're feeling nervous before engaging in some activity, she recommends categorizing those feelings not as harmful anxiety ("Oh no, I'm doomed!") but instead as helpful anticipation ("I'm energized and ready to go!").

Research shows the value of this technique. For example, students who were taking a math test achieved higher scores when they recategorized their anxiety as a sign that the body was coping. In another study, individuals were presented a series of tasks including singing karaoke and speaking in public. Participants were instructed to say "I am anxious," "I am excited," or nothing before singing or speaking. The "excited" participants sang better, and spoke more confidently and persuasively, than their counterparts.

At other times, negative feelings may be due to a temporary situation—and you must simply find a way to survive them.

For example, consider my friend Julia's recent experience.

As a clinical therapist, Julia's job is to help others deal effectively with their negative emotions. But she struggled to do
the same after a really bad day of her own. The unfortunate
events began when she was waiting in line to pay for parking at the mall—with her four-year-old in the back seat—and
another car backed into her. That led to an hour-and-a-half
phone call with her insurance company that evening, while
trying to put her children down to sleep. After finally getting
things organized and settled for the next day, and then getting
ready for bed, the toilet broke. She and her husband were up
until 1:30 a.m. trying to fix it. Julia eventually crawled into bed
at 2:00 a.m. with what she described as an "unsettled" feeling.

"Sometimes when I have a bad day I can laugh it off and
be fine with it all," said Julia. "But not this time. This time all
was not well.

"But spiraling down into a pity party, or blaming or crit-
icizing myself for having negative feelings, wasn't going
to do much good. So, instead of getting myself even more
worked up, and judging myself for letting relatively minute inconveniences throw me off, I took some deep breaths,
acknowledged and accepted the feelings, and reminded
myself that they, like everything else, would be temporary—
and that I would get through this."

Julia admitted that the feelings didn't go away completely
that night—but they didn't take over either.

"Some days are harder than others. But that's just the truth
for all of us. So instead of fighting that, or fighting ourselves,
we acknowledge and accept ourselves as humans who feel all
the feelings. And none of them are permanent, and we're not
weird, broken, or flawed for having them. Just human."

By acknowledging, accepting, and working through her
feelings, Julia turned "emotional" into "emotionally intelligent."

➤ **TRY THIS:** If you find yourself struggling with negative emotions, ask yourself: What is this feeling telling me? Can I use this emotion to motivate me to make a change? Or, can I find a way to get through the day, confident that things will be better tomorrow?

Six Surprising Ways to Build Emotional Intelligence

Researchers have found that some of our favorite recreational activities can increase our ability to understand and manage our emotions. Here are six surprising (and enjoyable) ways to sharpen your EQ.

1. Watch movies.

If you're a movie fan, you realize the emotional responses a good film can inspire—from eliciting sympathy for a tragically flawed character to feeling lifted by an inspirational story.

So, the next time you watch a film, take a few moments afterwards to reflect on the emotions you felt during different scenes. Ask yourself: How did this movie affect me, and why? Doing so will help you understand your own emotional reactions better.

2. Listen to music.

Music exercises great power over our emotions. The next time you start your playlist, pay attention to the feelings each song inspires, and try to determine why these songs resonate.

3. Read.

Recent studies suggest that reading fiction has a unique effect on the mind. As you delve into a story, you stretch your imagination to put yourself in the characters' shoes, to under-stand their thinking, their feelings, their motivations. This builds empathy that you can then use in your everyday life.

4. Engage in sports and exercise.

In a systematic review of thirty-six studies that assessed emotional intelligence in the context of athletics or physical activity, researchers found that higher emotional intelli-gence correlated with more successful physiological stress responses and psychological skill usage, as well as with more positive attitudes toward physical activity.

Additionally, the authors of the article stated that individ-uals who participated in the hard training and competitive pressure of sports demonstrated the ability to understand and regulate their emotions and those of other individuals.

5. Write.

More and more research suggests that writing, especially about traumatic or stressful events, serves as a form of catharsis, providing numerous benefits on individuals' emo-tional health.

6. Travel.

As one recent study demonstrated, extended travel can pro-mote increases in emotional stability, take individuals out of their comfort zone, and encourage growth in perspective.

Slowly but surely

To this day, Captain "Sully" Sullenberger insists that he's not a hero.

"As [my wife] likes to say, a hero is someone who risks his life running into a burning building," writes Sullenberger in his memoir. "Flight 1549 was different, because it was thrust upon me and my crew. We did our best, we turned to our training, we made good decisions, we didn't give up... and we had a good outcome. I don't know that 'heroic' describes that. It's more that we had a philosophy of life, and we applied it to the things we did that day, and the things we did on a lot of days leading up to it."

With the right preparation, this same philosophy can be applied to developing self-awareness and self-management.

In this chapter, we've discussed some exercises that can be used to strengthen your emotional muscles. Much as athletes must learn proper technique to excel at their sports, you must train your emotional abilities—by recognizing the power of your emotions and learning how to direct them in a way that's beneficial. But just as it takes time to master physical training techniques, you must be patient as you hone these mental and emotional skills.

Begin by focusing on just one or two of these methods at a time. Schedule time to sit and reflect, using the questions provided. Look for opportunities to incorporate them into your daily routine. Then, like the athlete, you must practice repeatedly, until you've internalized these habits and they become second nature.

As you gain skill and experience, you'll be able to combine techniques and methods to accomplish extraordinary emotional feats, transforming the strongest of your emotions from a destructive force to a power for good.

And while you may not call yourself a hero, you still might save the day.

3

Creatures of Habit

How Thoughts and Habits Affect Your Emotions

• • • • •

Watch your thoughts, they become words;
watch your words, they become actions;
watch your actions, they become habits;
watch your habits, they become character;
watch your character, for it becomes your destiny.

FRANK OUTLAW

ONE DAY, WHILE sitting on a park bench soaking up the sun, you observe a young father (we'll call him James) playing with his small children.

James's phone sounds a message alert. For the next few minutes, his attention shifts: he's busy reading and responding to a work email. The children grow impatient, begging for Dad to rejoin the game. "Just a second," he says, his eyes fixated on the phone. The children are insistent, their volume increasing with each successive call: "Daddy… Daddy… Daddy… "

Suddenly, James snaps. "I TOLD YOU TO WAIT A SEC-OND!" he yells. For a brief moment, the gentle and peaceful father transforms. His yell inspires fear and tears. He instantly puts his phone away to console the children, regretting taking it out in the first place.

The next day, the episode repeats itself.

A similar thing happens to a woman named Lisa. She heads toward the subway, ready for her evening commute after a long day. Suddenly, she's distracted by the sale signs at her favorite store and promises herself she'll go in "just for a look," knowing that a new outfit is not in the budget. Within minutes, she spots a pair of shoes she can't pass up. But she's also aware she's in severe debt and her credit card bills have steadily increased over the past several months.

"This is the last time," Lisa thinks, as the cashier swipes the card.

Then, there's Steve. After struggling for years to break his cigarette addiction, Steve feels like he's finally making progress. He's been off nicotine for a month, and his cravings are getting weaker.

But today has been a tough day at work. After a particularly difficult phone call with his manager, Steve sneaks over to his friend's stash, takes a cigarette, and heads outside. After lighting up, he immediately feels guilty.

Chances are you can identify with at least one of these stories. The circumstances or temptations specific to individuals may differ, but the behavior patterns are often similar, all leading to a single, inescapable truth: our emotions and our habits are inextricably linked.

Fact of life

When it comes to our emotional reactions, we all have weaknesses. We may have incorporated the pause into our everyday life, but we still send the occasional email we wish we could take back. We strive to listen to and respect alternative perspectives, until one of those perspectives challenges a value we deeply cherish.

These examples demonstrate just how difficult it can be to develop self-control, the ability to manage our thoughts, speech, and actions—especially in the midst of an emotionally charged situation.

Attempts to master a skill or competency usually go something like this: You learn the theory. You work to apply what you've learned. You practice over and over... and you begin to progress, eventually reaching a high level of competence. Of course, there will always be room for improvement—but if you look back at your trajectory, you can see definite signs of advancement. You're no Jimi Hendrix, but you're certainly a much better guitar player than a year ago.

Developing self-control is slower, and it's filled with more setbacks. Over time, you see slight improvement; then, an emotionally charged situation catches you off guard. You say something you later regret, which you find discouraging. Quickly, you regress to bad habits.

But why is cultivating self-control so difficult? Are we all merely victims, doomed to mindlessly repeat these behaviors throughout our lives?

In this chapter, I'll share some of the details behind the brain's emotional programming, explain how it relates to the growth mindset, and explore the process of changing habits. I'll also delve into the perils of the "emotional hijack" and teach you how to escape it. Finally, I'll examine the difference between proactive and reactive behavior—and show how the former can shape and mold the latter.

Through it all you'll discover that although changing life-long habits isn't necessarily easy, it *is* possible—and why doing so is worth the effort.

Rewiring the brain

The human brain is amazingly complex, and scientists are continuously striving to understand exactly how it works. But recent research has shed light on a remarkable characteristic of the human brain: its ability to change.

"For decades, neuroscientists assumed that the adult brain is essentially fixed in form and function," writes renowned neuroscientist Richard Davidson in his book *The Emotional Life of Your Brain*. "But we now know that this picture of a static, unchanging brain is wrong. Instead, the brain has a property called neuroplasticity, the ability to change its structure and function in significant ways. That change can come about in response to the experiences we have as well as to the thoughts we think."

Think about that for a second. Essentially, due to the brain's "plasticity," or ability to change, you actually have some authority over your own "programming," so to speak. Through concentrated thought and purposeful actions, you can influence the amount of control you exhibit over your emotional reactions and tendencies.

This philosophy harmonizes with the discoveries of Stanford psychology professor Carol Dweck. For years, Dweck has studied the self-conceptions people use to guide their behavior, to motivate themselves, and to build self-control. Through decades of experimentation, she has demonstrated that while you may be born with certain innate talents or aptitudes, it is experience, training, and personal effort that can help you become the person you want to become. "In [the growth] mindset, the hand you're dealt is just the starting point for development," explains Dweck in her bestselling book *Mindset*. "Everyone can change and grow through application and experience."

But when it comes to emotions, do you really *want* to attempt to control your emotional experience?

Let's consider a few circumstances to show why you should.

Escaping the emotional hijack

Have you ever felt that you're an unwilling slave to your emotions? As if you've been programmed to react a certain way to a specific set of circumstances, and there's simply nothing you can do about it?

One of the reasons we react in a certain way is that we're wired to respond habitually and emotionally to certain triggers. This reaction has to do with the amygdala, the part of the brain that's been referred to as our emotional processor.

The amygdala is a complex almond-shaped structure found deep inside the brain (ergo the name, derived from the Greek word *amygdale*, meaning "almond"), which is responsible for a wide range of cognitive and emotional functions. The brain actually has two amygdalae, one in each side (or hemisphere) of the brain. These structures play a large role in the processing of memories—specifically by attaching emotional significance to those memories. If you see a familiar face, for example, the amygdala goes to work: If it's a close friend, you'll feel a surge of joy. If it's someone who rubs you the wrong way, you'll feel the opposite.

While much of the decision-making process takes place in other parts of the brain (such as the prefrontal cortex), scientists recognize the amygdala's propensity to take over in certain circumstances.

For example, think back to James. As soon as he hears that email alert on his phone, he switches his focus. Physically, he may still be sitting next to his children—but his mind has returned to the office. As the children grow impatient, they accept the challenge: get Dad's attention back, by any means necessary. As the intensity of the children's pleas increase, the father becomes more and more annoyed—until he snaps. The result? An unfinished email, two crying children, and severe frustration for all parties.

This is a simple example of what Daniel Goleman calls an emotional hijacking (or hijack): a situation in which emotions overrule our typical thinking processes. We might liken the amygdala's action here to an emergency override of the mind, springing into action whenever we feel anxious or threatened and activating our fight, flight, or freeze response. The father wants to complete his task, and his children are suddenly try-ing to stop him from doing so. As the amygdala interprets this as a threat, it provokes an immediate and aggressive reaction.

Emotional hijacks can work to our advantage or disadvan-tage. In the case of a real emergency, the amygdala can give you the courage to defend your loved ones against an attacker who's bigger or stronger than you. But it can also move you to engage in risky, irrational, and even dangerous behavior in everyday situations.

Simply understanding how the amygdala works is an important step in identifying and learning from your own personal emotional hijacks, as well as developing strategies to deal with them. Of course, it would be great if you could identify your triggers ahead of time, but usually it will happen the other way around: you react to some stimulus and say or do something you later regret.

Now you're faced with a choice: You can forget what happened, move on, and react the same way the next time you're faced with similar circumstances. Or, you can try to sort through your thoughts and feelings, like pieces of a puzzle. As you begin to understand *why* you reacted the way you did, you can train your default reaction so you respond differently next time.

If you choose the second option, you can start the process by using these self-reflection questions to contemplate your behavior:

1 Why did I react the way I did?
2 Did my reaction help me or harm me?
3 How does this situation fit into the big picture? That is, how will I feel about it in hour? A week? A year?
4 What may I have misunderstood or be getting wrong, especially in the heat of the moment?
5 What would I change if I could do it again?
6 What could I say to myself next time that would help me think more clearly?

The goal of these questions is to get you thinking, so that you're more adept at recognizing your emotional behavior and tendencies moving forward. You can then take action to change those limiting or damaging behaviors.

So, what does this look like in real life?

Let's say that when driving a car, you have a tendency to get easily offended by fellow drivers. If another car comes too close or gets in your space, you take it personally. Before you know it, you're caught up in the moment, tailgating or looking for some other type of revenge so you can let the other driver know who's boss. Of course, because you're in the middle of an emotional hijack, your last concern is the possibility you could cause an accident or provoke a violent reaction.

Sometime later, though, you have an opportunity to cool down. You're thankful things didn't get out of hand, but you recognize that such behavior could get you into trouble in the future.

Using the questions on the previous page as a foundation, along with some of the tools from the previous chapter, you think over the situation. You then ask yourself the following:

· How would my opinion of a fellow driver change if I found out they were dealing with extenuating circumstances, like rushing a pregnant woman to the hospital or trying to get to an injured family member?
· What if the driver's actions were unintentional? Don't I make mistakes while driving? How would I want another person to act if I mistakenly cut them off?
· If I continue to retaliate against fellow drivers, how might they respond? How would this affect my family and me? Is it worth the risk?
· How does this incident fit into the big picture? Will I really care about a driver who cut me off an hour, week, or year later?

With these questions, your goal is to change how your brain processes these situations. If you no longer interpret fellow drivers' behavior as a personal attack, you'll engage the other parts of your brain when you get cut off, resulting in a more thoughtful and rational decision-making process.

Now, let's go back to James. He feels guilty for yelling at his kids and wishes to make a change. Upon reflection, he recognizes that he gets easily frustrated when trying to write emails while in the company of his children. Because of this, he decides to only respond to such messages at specific times. He silences the message notifications on his phone (or turns them off completely) so he's not tempted to look at every alert. And when the time comes to check email, he prepares his children by telling them: "Daddy needs a few minutes to take care of something for work." He then makes sure the children are occupied and supervised.

Engaging in this type of contemplative thought increases James's self-awareness and inspires further insights. In time, James realizes that pretty much any type of multitasking severely inhibits his ability to communicate effectively. Based on this realization, he works on becoming more focused. In the office, he puts away his phone so he can get more done, only checking it at specific times. He makes a concentrated effort to finish a task (or at least reach a good stopping point) before beginning another one. At home, when his wife attempts to start a conversation, he asks for a minute to finish what he's doing so he can give her his full attention.

James feels great about all of these changes. I know, because James is me. (Yup, James is my middle name.)

I decided to turn those emotional hijacks into a catalyst for intense thought and reflection. As I reevaluated who I was and where I was headed, I realized changes were needed.

I realized how dangerous my work had become—because I started to love it. I loved it so much it was all I ever wanted to do. If I was away from my computer for more than a couple of hours, I felt uncomfortable. As soon as I got an opportunity, it was back to business.

It's not who I wanted to become.

Since I made those changes some years ago, the results have been dramatic. I really enjoy my work, so the temptation to do too much is always there. It's a struggle to find balance and continue to see the big picture. (I'm not perfect. My wife helps a lot.) But I feel more emotionally connected with my wife and children than ever. I'm more productive at work, and my focus has improved dramatically. Those simple changes have made me a better husband, father, and worker.

The moral of the story: emotional hijacks aren't pleasant, but they're inevitable. The question is: What are you going to do with them? With the right strategy, you can make them work for you, instead of against you.

However, it's important to realize that these types of adjustments don't happen overnight. As the saying goes, old habits die hard.

Designing your habits: Becoming proactive instead of reactive

Another factor affecting our personal "programming" has to do with the habits we form.

"Habits, scientists say, emerge because the brain is constantly looking for ways to save effort," writes Charles Duhigg, author of the bestselling book *The Power of Habit*. When our brains are more efficient, we don't have to constantly think about basic behaviors like walking or talking, which allow us to use our mental energy for other tasks. (This is why, for example, we go on autopilot when we're brushing our teeth or parallel parking.) When the brain identifies that a particular behavioral routine leads to a reward, it often gives birth to a habit.

The problem, though, is the brain can't tell the difference between good rewards and bad ones. Lisa, the young woman mentioned above, doesn't walk into the store because she *needs* a new outfit; she does so because she's established a habit—one that provides an emotional reward by satisfying her curiosity. Similarly, although Steve desperately wants to quit smoking, he continues to relapse when under severe stress. His brain has become wired to seek relief through the nicotine buzz he gets from a cigarette.

Your vice may be different. You enjoy staying up late watching Netflix, but this leads to chronic sleep deprivation, which

We are what we repeatedly do. Excellence is not an act, but a habit.

WILL DURANT

adversely affects your mood. Or maybe you fool yourself into trying to knock out one more task when you should be leaving for your next appointment. This results in you racing against the clock, adding unnecessary stress to your day.

As challenging as it can be to break bad habits, the truth is that you don't have to be at their mercy. Scientists have discovered that habits won't simply go away on their own, but they can be replaced. That means you're not doomed to mindlessly repeat your current routine just because it's what you've done for years. Instead, you can rewire your brain by designing your own habits.

For example, consider the work of therapist Brent Atkinson. After years of conducting weekly therapy sessions with various couples, Atkinson realized that even the romantic partners who developed profound insights regarding their behavior repeatedly fell into "the same old patterns." He attributes this to his clients' personal experiences.

"Brain studies suggest that across their lifetimes, people develop internal mechanisms for coping with things that are upsetting to them," explains Atkinson. "The brain organizes these coping mechanisms into coherent, self-protective neural response programs that are highly automated. Once a neural response program forms, each time it is triggered, a predictable pattern of thoughts, urges and actions unfold. Neural response programs can dramatically bias people's perceptions and interpretations without them realizing it... generating powerful inclinations to attack, defend, or retreat."

In other words, the way you respond when you become upset is a habit your mind has created to protect itself, which it has already repeated thousands of times. (Many married couples have arguments so predictable they seem to follow a script.) The key to interrupting this cycle is to recondition the way you respond in these situations.

Atkinson and his colleagues helped clients achieve this by teaching them to think more flexibly when under stress. They instructed clients to ask their spouses to speak into a voice recorder on their smartphone whenever they felt dissatisfied with or disapproving of their partner's behavior, "as if [they] were leaving a voice mail message for [their] partner."

Later, those therapists would play those recordings for their clients with the goal of helping them do the following:

- Identify the internal reactions that arise as they listen to their partners' complaints.
- Consider how they would ideally react in such moments.
- Repetitively practice a new way of thinking and responding when they become annoyed or upset.

The results were remarkable, with clients quickly learning to slow down their thinking and change the way they respond when under stress. "For many clients, this is the first time in their lives that they've paid close attention to what happens internally when they feel criticized," says Atkinson.

So, how can you adapt these lessons to your personal circumstances?

➤ TRY THIS: To attempt to change your habitual responses, practice the following three-step method.

1. Motivate.

Atkinson points out that anyone desiring to change their habits must be properly motivated. "They must be convinced that their current habits are in serious need of revision and really want to change them," he writes.

So, find your motivation. Do you want to live longer? Do better at work? Enjoy a better quality of life?

By taking time to see how your habits can help or hinder you from achieving those goals, you may be able to muster up the motivation you need to make major change.

2. Practice.

To master a new skill, you must practice it over and over until it is internalized.

You could use Atkinson's suggestion to have your partner record a "complaining voice mail" that you then play for yourself at a later time. But if you're unlikely to do that, you could take advantage of another situation: the next time you're reading the news or scrolling through social media, seek out comments or opinions you feel passionately about. Don't respond to these; instead, pay attention to your internal thoughts as you listen or read. Ask yourself the six self-reflection questions mentioned on page 43. Finally, use your imagination to review and revisualize a situation in which you previously had trouble; then, mentally rehearse how you plan to handle similar circumstances in the future.

Remember the comparison to a professional athlete: just as these competitors practice their technique thousands of times before performing on the big stage, you can train the mental processes you need to engage before encountering the next emotionally charged moment.

3. Apply.

Despite countless hours of practice, athletes gain invaluable experience from performing in real-world competition. It's there—in the arena or stadium—that contestants put their skills to work.

You, too, will have plenty of opportunities to apply what you've practiced. Every day presents multiple emotionally charged moments—a discussion with an irate colleague or family member; an alluring temptation.

My personal experience in applying these methods is that I now encounter fewer emotional hijacks than previously. But additionally, once a hijack begins, I'm often able to identify it, step back, and prevent it from exploding into a full-blown catastrophe. In these cases, a sincere apology for my initial reaction quickly defuses the situation. It's then much easier for me and anyone else involved to calm down, and it makes moving forward more productive and pleasant for everyone.

Don't expect to build self-control overnight. But if you continue integrating "habits by design" every chance you get, you can proactively shape your emotional reactions. As a result, you'll become battle-hardened and better equipped to deal with the most severe emotional challenges.

Don't give up!

Make no mistake: attempting to change your emotional behavior is no easy task. Many times, you will be dealing with neural connections you have taken a lifetime to develop. Even after moving forward, expect to take a few steps back. At times, you may wonder if you're really making any progress.

The truth is, none of us can control our emotions perfectly. We all make mistakes, and we'll continue to do so. Show me an "expert" in emotional intelligence, and I'll show you another person who loses their temper or makes an emotionally faulty decision—under the wrong circumstances.

But if you treat those hijacks as case studies into your own behavior, they become remarkable learning experiences. Strive to identify which events triggered your response and which deeply ingrained habits may have contributed to it. Use your imagination to review and rehearse. Look for ways to replace bad habits with good ones. Finally, practice, practice, practice.

In doing so, you can gradually "reprogram" your brain's instinctive reactions—and cultivate the habits you need to successfully keep your emotions in balance.

4

Diamonds in the Rough

Why You Should Treat All Feedback as a Gift

• • • • •

He only profits from praise who values criticism.

HEINRICH HEINE

AS A YOUNG boy, Thomas Keller often helped out in the kitchen of the Palm Beach restaurant managed by his mother. He eventually developed a love for cooking that would inspire him to pursue a career as a chef. After achieving countless accolades and winning numerous prestigious awards, Keller developed a reputation as one of the most skilled culinary artists in the world.

This explains why Pete Wells, the lead restaurant critic for the *New York Times*, made headlines when he published a harsh criticism of Keller's New York eatery Per Se. Wells described his three dining experiences at Per Se (between fall and winter 2015) as "respectably dull at best to disappointingly flatfooted at worst." He pulled no punches in using words like "random," "flavorless," "purposeless," and "rubbery" to describe the dishes he sampled.

So how would Keller, a noted perfectionist and honored chef, respond to being thoroughly bashed—by the same newspaper, incidentally, that named Per Se "the best restaurant in New York City" just four years earlier?

He apologized.

In a statement that is equal parts humble and inspiring, Keller accepted responsibility for Per Se's poor performance and promised improvement.

"We pride ourselves on maintaining the highest standards, but we make mistakes along the way," Keller admitted in a statement on his website. "We are sorry we let you down."

In an interview with *Town & Country* magazine several months later, Keller acknowledged that he didn't view Wells's review as a personal attack. "Maybe we were complacent," he said. "I learned that, maybe, as a team we were a little bit too arrogant, our egos too exposed."

Soon after the *Times* review debuted, Keller traveled to a handful of restaurants he owns to meet with the 1029 staff members and deliver an explanation. The only way to diminish the impact of the review, Keller said, would be one guest at a time.

In the world of fine dining, where top chefs are deified, Keller's response was a breath of fresh air. At the same time, it revealed on a larger stage what many closer associates of Keller saw as a major strength of character: his ability to benefit from negative feedback.

Why we all need feedback

Before you dismiss Keller's statement as an insincere PR move, consider how difficult this action is in reality: to accept harsh, negative feedback, swallow your pride, and apologize.

Grant Achatz, an award-winning chef who worked for four years under Keller at his acclaimed California restaurant the French Laundry, described how this type of reaction is built in to his former mentor's DNA.

"When something like this happens... he immediately reacts in a positive fashion and tries to make it better," said Achatz. "We can speculate about his ego or arrogance, but it is not who he is."

If you're anything like me, you can quickly think of similar situations when your response to criticism has not been so gracious.

It's not difficult to understand why. We're all emotionally attached to our work, beliefs, and opinions. Sure, we might *claim* that we want to learn and improve, to be the best version of ourselves. But when the time comes for someone to tell us how, we get tense. Sensitive. Upset.

But what if you learned to view criticism differently? What if you found a way to transform the effect of those comments from attack to something of value?

We might compare the feedback we receive to an unpolished diamond. To the untrained eye, a freshly mined gem may not look valuable, or even attractive. But after the long and complex process of sorting, cutting, and polishing, its true value becomes obvious. In a similar way, learning to extract the benefits of criticism can prove to be an invaluable skill.

Of course, the feedback you receive won't always be critical. A well-timed compliment or bit of flattery may bring a smile to your face. But even sincere praise can be detrimental in the long run if you don't learn how to view it in the right way.

So, how can you get the most from others' feedback?

That's the question we'll answer in this chapter. I'll also show you how others' comments can affect you in ways you may not even notice. I'll then outline what type of feedback is most beneficial and share some tips to help make sure you get it.

Feedback is a gift

"Inside Amazon: Wrestling Big Ideas in a Bruising Workplace."

That was the title of an infamous article published by the *New York Times* in 2015. The story portrayed e-commerce behemoth Amazon as a brutal employer that put innovation and company performance above the well-being of its people.

"At Amazon, workers are encouraged to tear apart one another's ideas in meetings, toil long and late . . . and [are] held to standards that the company boasts are 'unreasonably high,'" opened the article. According to the writers, sabotage and Machiavellian behavior were common. Former and current Amazon employees shared stories of managers who showed callous indifference to workers' serious health problems or family tragedies.

"Nearly every person I worked with, I saw cry at their desk," said one former employee.

The story quickly went viral. Former employees shared experiences both good and bad. (Consider that Amazon employs more than three hundred thousand people worldwide.) The article drew nearly six thousand comments on the *New York Times* website and even sparked a public debate between a senior executive from Amazon and the *Times*'s executive editor, which played out on *Medium*, the popular blogging platform.

But in the media frenzy that followed, a single man's response to the backlash stood out.

On the same weekend the article was published, Amazon founder and CEO Jeff Bezos sent out a memo to Amazon employees. In it, he encouraged them to give the *New York Times* article "a careful read."

The criticism surely stung. "I don't recognize this Amazon, and I very much hope you don't either," Bezos told employees in the memo, adding that the *Times* story "[didn't] describe the Amazon I know or the caring Amazonians I work with every day." He directed employees to report any incidents similar to those in the story. Bezos even invited employees to reach out to him directly through email.

"Even if it's rare or isolated, our tolerance for any such lack of empathy needs to be zero," wrote Bezos.

No doubt, Bezos felt a flurry of emotions as he pondered how to deal with a sudden crisis. Nonetheless, he used the negative feedback as a catalyst—to reevaluate the current situation at his company and to convey how seriously he took the allegations.

Did anything result from this compelling call to action? In 2016 the company announced significant changes to how it would assess employees moving forward. In an official statement, the new process was described as "radically simplified," maintaining a new focus on employee strengths as opposed to "the absence of weaknesses."

Bezos's memo, much like Thomas Keller's initial response to the harsh review, vividly illustrates the legitimate benefits that result when we view criticism as an opportunity to learn.

But this type of response isn't so common—and it's easy to understand why.

When it comes to your work, you've invested blood, sweat, and sometimes tears. So, it's natural to feel a degree of pain when others devalue that effort. Added is the fact that your personal beliefs, convictions, and values make up so much of your identity. *Attack these, and you attack me*, is often the default reaction.

It's even worse when the critique comes from a friend, spouse, or family member. *How could they*, you ask yourself. *They're supposed to be on my side!*

But here's the thing: nobody's right all the time. You need others to expose your blind spots, to point out what you're missing, because that's how you improve.

Unfortunately, much of the criticism we receive is delivered in a way that's less than ideal. Sometimes it's downright brutal—even wrong, in many ways. But even if it's not delivered constructively, criticism should still be considered a gift—because most criticism is rooted in truth, meaning there's something you can take away from it, some insight you can use to improve yourself.

And even if criticism is completely off base, it's still extremely valuable because it helps you understand the perspective of those who see the world differently than you. Learning from another person's views and rationale can even help you focus your own thinking and refine your beliefs and values.

By viewing negative feedback as a learning opportunity, you can do the following:

· Confirm the validity of your ideas and prepare yourself for similar criticism in the future.
· Better craft your message in a way that reaches those with varying perspectives.
· Better identify your target audience.
· Change and adapt when appropriate.

Of course, I'm not excusing criticism that's hurtful or thoughtless. If you need to deliver negative feedback, doing so with respect and tact is not only the kind thing to do, it will get you better results. (More on this later in the book.)

But if you're on the receiving end of criticism, you don't have that luxury. Remember that feedback is like a freshly mined diamond: it may not look pretty, but it has great potential for value. Now it's time to cut and polish, learn, and grow.

Turning negative into positive

In order to benefit from negative feedback, it's important to remember that anything you see as a threat is going to spring your amygdala into action, bypassing your normal decision-making process. This circumvention manifests itself in a number of ways: You may tense up and stop listening. Or, you may automatically begin to justify or rationalize what you've said or done. You may even attempt to minimize the problem or shift blame to someone else.

These actions don't benefit anyone. But how do you keep your emotions from getting in the way?

The key is to train yourself to view criticism not as a personal attack, but instead as a learning opportunity.

➤ **TRY THIS:** Whenever you receive negative feedback, focus on answering two questions:

- Putting my personal feelings aside, what can I learn from this alternate perspective?

- How can I use this feedback to help me improve?

By considering these questions, you shift your time and energy to a productive exercise. In effect, you turn what could be a negative situation into a positive experience—a chance to learn and better yourself.

Granted, this isn't easy in the beginning. Your natural response to criticism is most likely a knee-jerk reaction, a habit that was years in the making. But if you take time to answer these questions, even if it's several hours after initially receiving feedback, you'll still be able to learn. And if you do this consistently, you'll find that your natural reaction to criticism gradually changes.

I learned this lesson the hard way. In an early leadership role many years ago, I experienced an exchange I'll never forget. I chastised a team member—we'll call him David—for a major blunder. My point was valid, but I'm sure I could have delivered it better.

David's response was quick and cutting: "You know, you're the kind of manager the rest of us hate."

Ouch.

Of course, David could have delivered his message more tactfully. But there was no use dwelling on that; there was value in David's perspective. I took his words to heart, asked him why he felt the way he did, and learned from his honesty. In the end, it made me a better manager—and it showed David that I wasn't the jerk that he thought.

A word of caution, though: be careful not to dwell excessively on negative feedback.

Doing so could paralyze you or cause you to become crushed by the comments of naysayers—to the point that it makes you feel like giving up. You may get distracted from your priorities and values. Or, you may get so caught up in the pursuit of proving others wrong that you lose sight of your strengths and waste time and effort trying to become something you're not.

When others point out potential blind spots, your goal should be to learn and move on. Most of the feedback you get from others will be subjective, so keep that in mind, too. Additionally, during times when your self-esteem is especially low, you may find it beneficial to focus more on what you're doing right than on areas for improvement.

Finally, there are certain occasions when you should completely shut out criticism from others. If you determine that someone is trying to harm you or destroy your sense of self-worth, don't give it any thought. Instead, seek feedback from those whom you know you can trust and who have your best interests at heart.

A balanced view of praise

It's vital to keep your emotions in check when receiving criticism, but how about when you're praised or commended?

There are innumerable benefits to giving sincere, specific praise to others, and we'll explore these in detail in later chapters. When you're on the receiving end, praise can help you identify your strengths, build self-esteem and confidence in your abilities, and provide much-needed motivation.

But there's potential danger to getting your ears tickled, so to speak. Allowing your emotions to run wild after receiving praise could lead you to overestimate your abilities, to become careless, brash, even arrogant. You might start to look down on others or develop a sense of entitlement.*

You should also consider if all the adulation you're receiving is authentic or if there's an ulterior motive. Whereas praise may be given out of a sincere desire to show appreciation, flattery is often motivated by selfishness. "The most common form of manipulation comes packaged in the form of flattery—it's also the most dangerous," writes leadership advisor Mike Myatt in his bestselling book *Hacking Leadership*. "The problem with the old saying that 'flattery will get you everywhere'

---

* For example, in 2015 Dutch researchers published a study revealing that children who were praised excessively by their parents scored higher on qualities associated with narcissism. "People with high self-esteem think they're as good as others, whereas narcissists think they're better than others," said Brad Bushman, co-author of the study and professor of communication and psychology at Ohio State University.

is that those with less than pure intentions not only believe it, they act on it. The lazy, the power hungry, the greedy, the gravy-trainers, the psychopaths and sociopaths all understand that flattery is *not* harmless. Quite to the contrary, these sooth-sayers understand that flattery has the power to influence, corrupt, undermine and deceive... Manipulation in the form of flattery is little more than a covert form of aggression."

He that loves to be flattered is worthy o' the flatterer.

WILLIAM SHAKESPEARE, *TIMON OF ATHENS*

So, beware of individuals who praise only those who can benefit them. Rather, appreciate praise and commendation as tools to help you identify your strengths and build on them. Use praise as motivation to work hard and consistently improve. At the same time, keep in mind that every ability, skill, or talent you possess is the result of what you've received from others. This will help you resist the temptation to overly inflate your view of self or put yourself on a pedestal, which only sets you up for a fall.

➤ **TRY THIS:** The next time someone commends you, thank them politely. Later, ask yourself the following:

- What can I learn from their commendation? How can I repeat what I did right?

- Who helped me perform well? Can I, in turn, thank or praise them, too?

- Was the person's praise sincere, or was it an attempt to flatter or get something in return?

How to get the feedback you need

"I realize I need feedback to grow," you say. "But what if no one wants to give it to me?"

There are plenty of reasons why it can be difficult to draw out valuable feedback. At work, your boss or colleagues may not consider this type of communication a priority. Or they may find the idea intimidating, afraid of how the other person might react. If *you're* the boss, your team may fear the consequences of giving you negative feedback.

At home, a lack of feedback can gradually destroy your relationships. Instead of engaging in much-needed conversation, many family members are content to spend hours reading, watching TV, or playing games on their mobile devices. Despite sitting or lying just a few feet away from each other, their minds are worlds apart.

But there's a simple way to get the feedback you desperately need: ask for it.

None of us do this as much as we should. For example, when's the last time you asked your spouse, child, or colleague to share something they appreciate about you? Or tell you something they wish you would improve? It certainly takes courage to ask those questions... but imagine what you could do with the answers.

When you regularly seek feedback, others become more inclined to tell you what they really think, thereby increasing your opportunities to learn. But there's another benefit—a hidden one—to asking others to share their opinions: people tend to think highly of those who consistently ask for critical feedback.

"Someone who's asking for coaching is more likely to take what is said to heart and genuinely improve," write Sheila Heen and Douglas Stone, co-authors of *Thanks for the Feedback: The Science and Art of Receiving Feedback Well.* "But also because when you ask for feedback, you not only find out how others see you, you also *influence* how they see you. Soliciting constructive criticism communicates humility, respect, passion for excellence, and confidence, all in one go."

Of course, communication is a two-way street. You need to tell these same people what you appreciate about them, as well as what needs you have that aren't being fulfilled. (More about how to deliver this type of feedback in chapter seven.)

But is it really that simple? Is getting helpful, effective feedback really just about asking for it?

While asking for direct feedback can lead to great discoveries, you also need to consider your technique.

➤ **TRY THIS:** Heen and Stone advise against using vague questions like: "Do you have any feedback for me?" Rather, narrow your focus. For example, at work you could ask a colleague, boss, or direct report: "What's one thing you see me doing (or failing to do) that holds me back?"*

---

* In a separate interview, Heen advocates the same technique to help critique your performance in a specific situation. For example, you could ask: "What's one thing I could have done better in that meeting or presentation?"

"That person may name the first behavior that comes to mind or the most important one on his or her list," the authors write. "Either way, you'll get concrete information and can tease out more specifics at your own pace."

At home, you might consider asking your partner or another family member: "What's one thing you feel I could improve in our relationship? You know, a bad habit you wish I'd change, or a set of circumstances I could handle better?"

This type of question might come as a surprise at first, so give the other person a chance to think about it and come back to you. Of course, you also have to brace yourself for what's coming. But since you're the one seeking the feedback, it's easier to keep the end goal in mind—namely, improving yourself or your relationship.

How Great Organizations Benefit from Feedback

All companies say they value transparency and honesty. Most are lying.

A truly transparent company—one that encourages open and honest communication from all employees—is hard to find. Instead, in most organizations you'll find a complex web of office politics. Employees have limited access to managers and team leads; those who do are often hesitant to share critical opinions, for fear that they will be black-balled, demoted, or even dismissed.

If you hold a position of leadership, here's a two-step method to build true transparency in your organization.

1. Prove it—by rewarding honest feedback.

Instead of building echo chambers and promoting group-think, encourage your people to express opposing view-points and opinions. Then, reward them for doing so. Some companies encourage submitting ideas for improve-ment through a "suggestion box" (physical or electronic), offering cash or other bonuses to those whose ideas are implemented.

2. Focus on content, not delivery.

If you're on the receiving end of a critical message, don't waste time thinking about the delivery.

A longtime employee at one organization made headlines when he submitted an especially critical exit interview—by hitting reply all to the thousands of employees. The com-pany chairman chastised the employee, later making the statement: "I would love to have received that criticism in a more constructive way because it does make you think. Should I have communicated more frequently? That's a valid point."

Remember, even if negative feedback is unfounded, it still provides a valuable window into the perspective of others.

So, if you're a manager or executive, encourage every employee to share their thoughts as if today were their last day on the job.

Find your diamonds

No one enjoys being told they're wrong. But just as it takes skill and insight to see the exquisite beauty in an unpolished diamond, you must look beyond the surface of others' comments to extract true value.

External feedback allows you to see yourself from other perspectives and expose blind spots. It helps you understand your strengths so you can work to maximize them, and it helps you identify your weaknesses so you can deal with them head-on.

As Walt Disney famously put it: "You may not realize it when it happens, but a kick in the teeth may be the best thing in the world for you."

The need for feedback is why the most successful companies in the world bring in outside consultants, and why scientists submit research to their peers for review. It's why a world-class chef like Thomas Keller pays attention to a harsh review. And it's why even the most talented athletes in the world have a coach.

The ability to process feedback effectively is vital because it allows you to expand your horizons and learn from others' experiences. That's true regardless of your age or gender, and it applies across roles—partner or parent, from CEO to entry-level employee.

So, when someone's willing to share their thoughts, consider it a gift. Process it. Ponder it. Accept it. Learn from it. Whether it's negative or positive, don't let it define you. Take what you can and move on.

And remember: although we're generally drawn to like-minded people, it's those who disagree with us—the ones who call us out, who point out our weaknesses and flaws—who help us grow. Those who challenge us truly make us better.

5

The Truth about Empathy
The Good, the Bad, and the Misunderstood

• • • • •

Don't judge a person until you've walked a mile in their shoes.

ANONYMOUS

IN 2008 I was planning a wedding with the love of my life, who lived in Germany. Life was grand.

I'd spent ten years with a nonprofit in New York; I loved the job and was being considered for a new position. But as my fiancée and I began preparing for our new life together, my situation took a turn. Due to a reorganization, my office needed to reduce personnel. My job was no longer secure, and my fiancée and I began talking seriously about me moving to Germany. We decided that if I made it through the next round of job cuts, she would join me in New York. If not, I would move.

I was told to expect a letter with the final decision within four to six weeks.

Six weeks came and went. Then, seven.

And eight.

Nine...

I wasn't sure how much longer I could take the suspense. I didn't even care anymore if they let me go; I just needed to know *something*. I called HR, trying my best to get any information I could, to no avail.

Eventually, I decided to take a different route.

I wrote an email directly to Mr. Pierce, the head of personnel, who was also on the executive board. My email was respectful but direct. I explained my situation, along with the fact that I was traveling to Germany in a few days to see my fiancée. I described how great it would be to open the letter with her in person.

Our organization had about six thousand staff members at the time, and I had never met Mr. Pierce—so I knew the chance was pretty good that my email would get buried in his inbox.

But after what had seemed like the longest two-and-a-half months of my life, it took two days after sending that message to receive a decision.

The day after I sent the email, I boarded a plane to Germany—and less than twelve hours later, my fiancée and I opened the letter together.

"You're going to love New York," I told her.

Easy to crave, hard to show

When Mr. Pierce read that email all those years ago, he was able to see beyond the request of a random junior manager. He was reading the deep concerns and feelings of one of his people. The problem was important to me, so it was important to him.

This example helps us understand the quality of empathy, the ability to see and feel things from another person's perspective.

We often hear about the need for more empathy in the world. No doubt you've witnessed this in one form or another: The manager who can't relate to the struggles of his team, and vice versa. Husbands and wives who no longer understand each other. The parent who has forgotten what teenage life is like... and the teen who can't see how much his parents care.

Or, just look online. Check the comments of any story and you'll find dozens of people, if not hundreds, launching verbal attacks at people they've never met. These aren't just differences of opinion; it's a barrage of insults, name-calling, even threats.

But if we all crave for others to try to see things from our perspective, why is it so hard for us to do the same?

In this chapter, you'll learn why empathy is often misunderstood and explore the challenges involved in developing it. We'll take a closer look at the practical ways empathy helps you in daily life, but also at how it can hurt you. Finally, we'll outline practical steps to help you achieve empathy in the right amount, which will strengthen your relationships and increase your effectiveness in almost any task.

What empathy is (and what it's not)

The English word "empathy" has existed for only about a century. But to discover the roots of this concept, we have to go back much further.

The Chinese philosopher Confucius, who lived over 2500 years ago, taught to "never impose on others what you would not choose for yourself." Hundreds of years later, Christians in the first century reading the New Testament were encouraged to "rejoice with people who rejoice, weep with people who weep" and "to suffer with one another."

Today, you'll get different definitions for empathy, depending on who you ask. But most would agree to some variation of the following: empathy is the ability to understand and share the thoughts or feelings of another.

To feel and display empathy, it's not necessary to share the same experiences or circumstances as others. Rather, empathy is an attempt to better understand the other person by getting to know their perspective.

Psychologists Daniel Goleman and Paul Ekman break down the concept of empathy into the following three categories.

Cognitive empathy is the ability to understand how a person feels and what they might be thinking. Cognitive empathy makes us better communicators, because it helps us relay information in a way that best reaches the other person.

Emotional empathy (also known as affective empathy) is the ability to share the feelings of another person. Some have described it as "your pain in my heart." This type of empathy helps you build emotional connections with others.

Compassionate empathy (also known as empathic concern) goes beyond simply understanding others and sharing their feelings: it actually moves us to take action, to help however we can.

To illustrate how these three branches of empathy work together, imagine that a friend has recently lost a close family member. Your natural reaction may be sympathy, a feeling of pity, or sorrow. Sympathy may move you to express condolences or to send a card—and your friend may appreciate these actions.

But showing empathy takes more time and effort. It begins with cognitive empathy: imagining what the person is going through. Who did they lose? How close were they to this person? Besides feelings of pain and loss, how will their life now change?

Empathy involves feeling your pain in my heart.

Emotional empathy will help you not only understand your friend's feelings, but share them somehow. You try to connect with something in yourself that knows the feeling of deep sorrow and emotional pain. You might remember how it felt when you lost someone close, or imagine how you *would* feel if you haven't had that experience.

Finally, compassionate empathy moves you to take action. You might provide a meal, so your friend doesn't need to worry about cooking. You could offer to help make necessary phone calls or do some chores around the house. Maybe you could go over to help keep them company; or, if they need to be alone, you could pick up the children and watch them for a while.

This is just one example of how empathy works, but every day will bring new opportunities to develop this trait. In fact, every interaction you share with another person is a chance to see things from a different perspective, to share their feelings, and to help.

Building Cognitive Empathy

Learning to think and feel from another person's perspective isn't simple. It's easy to misinterpret physical movements and facial expressions; a smile can mean joy or exuberance, but it can also signal sadness—or a host of other emotions. But building cognitive empathy is about making educated guesses, and the following exercises can help you hone this ability.

You are constantly interacting with other people—at work, at home, even when shopping or running errands. Before you engage with another person, consider what you know about their point of view. Ask yourself the following:

- How old is the other person? What's their family situation?
- Where did they grow up? What's their background?
- What's their occupation?
- How is their health?
- Who are their friends? Whom do they admire? What are their goals, wants, and desires?
- What do they know about the topic you're discussing? What don't they know? How do they feel about it?
- How would I feel in their shoes?
- How might they think or feel differently than I do?
- How might they respond to whatever I have to say?

Regardless of how effectively you answer these questions, your interpretation of another person's mood, behavior, or thinking will be influenced by your prior experience, so it's important to realize that your instincts may be wrong. That's also why it's important to take time after you engage with others to ponder your interaction, using questions like the following:

- Did things go well? Why or why not?
- What about their reaction went as I expected? What surprised me?
- What did they like or dislike?
- What did I learn about the other person?

Consider any type of feedback your communication partner provides (written, verbal, body language) to help you learn from the experience. Doing so will help you better understand not only others and their personalities, but also how they perceive your thoughts and communication style.

A roadblock to empathy

We yearn for everyone we have dealings with to consider our perspective and feelings. But why do we often fail to do the same for them? For one thing, it takes time and effort to understand how and why others feel the way they do. And frankly, we aren't willing to invest those resources for too many people.

But even when we're motivated to show empathy—in fact, even when we think we *are* showing empathy—our vision may not be as clear as we think it is.

In his bestselling book *Give and Take*, organizational psychologist Adam Grant cites an experiment led by Northwestern University psychologist Loran Nordgren, in which participants predicted how painful it would be to sit in a freezing room for five hours. A first group made their predictions while holding an arm in a bucket of warm water. A second group did so while holding an arm in a bucket of ice water.

As you might guess, the people with arms in cold water expected to feel the most pain.

But there was a third group, who also stuck one of their arms in a bucket of ice water. These participants then took their arm out and waited ten minutes before estimating how painful it would be to sit in the freezing room.

The result? Their predictions were identical to those in the warm-water group.

The third group had experienced ice-cold temperatures just ten minutes earlier, but as soon as they were no longer exposed to that degree of pain, they couldn't effectively remember it.

Psychologists refer to this as an empathy or perspective gap. "When we're not experiencing a psychologically or physically intense state," explains Grant, "we dramatically underestimate how much it will affect us."

The perspective gap explains why physicians consistently miss the mark when attempting to estimate their patients' level of pain, or why we find it so difficult to put ourselves in the shoes of our spouse or a family member. We tend to misjudge our own behavior and preferences depending on what state we are currently in. And even when we've experienced a situation similar to the person with whom we're trying to empathize, we remember dealing with those circumstances much better than we actually did.

Psychologist and behavioral economist George Loewenstein has studied these gaps in perception for years. He points out another way they affect us: by exaggerating our sense of willpower. "When we are dealing with our vices, we are shortsighted, impulsive and make ridiculous sacrifices to satisfy [them]," said Loewenstein in an interview. "But when we see other people succumbing to their vices, we think, 'How pathetic.'"

I recognized the truth of this firsthand some time ago.

For years my wife had a habit that grated on my nerves like no other: she would remove a full trash bag from our kitchen bin without replacing it. I absolutely despised coming to that bin with a handful of trash only to find there was no liner inside. I begged and pleaded, to no avail. There was always an excuse—distracted by the kids, in a rush to get out of the house.

How can she be so inconsiderate? I would think to myself. *Doesn't she care about my simple request? Aren't my feelings important enough to her?* I just couldn't understand it.

Then, one day, I had an epiphany.

My wife equally can't stand it when I leave the dinner table without taking my plate to the kitchen. Over the years, she asked me countless times to take my plate away as soon as I was done eating, so I wouldn't forget. I usually responded with an assurance that I'd do it in "just a few minutes."

One evening, I came across our dining room table an hour after we had finished eating. It was completely clear—except for a single, dirty plate.

At that moment it hit me: I was just as guilty as my wife.

I apologized for my habit of leaving dirty dishes on the table and promised to change. I made it a priority, and my wife noticed. So much so that she made a change of her own: that's right, she started replacing the trash bag.

You might consider this example trivial. But the lesson went much further than a couple of household chores.

Learning to identify perspective gaps is important because when a home or workplace lacks empathy, relationships deteriorate. Both parties wonder, *How in the world could anyone ever think or do that?* They remain fixated on the other person's failings instead of finding a way to relate. The result is a mental and emotional standoff where everyone sticks to their guns, no problems get solved, and situations appear to be irreconcilable.

But taking the initiative to show empathy can break the cycle.

When a person feels understood, they are more likely to reciprocate the effort and attempt to understand the other side. In time, this type of exchange builds a trusting relationship where both parties are motivated to give the other person the benefit of the doubt and forgive minor failings.

It's all about answering the question: How can I see things through the eyes of the other person?

To do so, you must work to increase awareness of your own biases and limited perspective. You can still draw on your own experiences, but you must go further.

> **TRY THIS:** The next time you struggle to see something from another person's point of view, strive to remember the following:

- You don't have the whole picture. At any given time, a person is dealing with many factors of which you're unaware.

- The way you think and feel about a situation may be very different from one day to the next, influenced by various elements, including your current mood.

- Under emotional stress, you may behave very differently than you think you would.

Keeping these points in mind will affect how you view the other person and influence how you deal with them. And since each of us goes through our own struggle at one point or another, it's only a matter of time before you'll need that same level of understanding.

The next level

Learning to bridge gaps in perception and relate to the experiences of others is important to developing cognitive empathy—the ability to understand what a person is thinking and feeling.

But to achieve emotional empathy requires going further. The goal is to actually share the feelings of the other person, leading to a deeper connection.

For example, consider Ray, who owns a small business.

Vera, Ray's office manager, has recently told him that she feels overwhelmed. In addition to her normal responsibilities, she's struggling to cover the tasks of a key employee who is on extended leave. She describes the daily routine as "relentless."

As Ray listens to Vera, he initially feels disappointed. Before hiring Vera he managed the office himself, so he knows how hard it can be. But he's also endured more challenging circumstances for a much longer period.

"She has nothing to complain about," Ray thinks to himself. "Why can't she just push through?"

In this situation, it's possible that Ray is suffering from a perspective gap. But it's not necessarily the case; it could be that Vera simply isn't capable of living up to Ray's expectations—at least, not in this current set of circumstances.

But this situation presents Ray with an opportunity to display emotional empathy—to focus on Vera's feelings instead of on her situation.

Vera says she feels overwhelmed. So, Ray asks himself: *When was a time I felt overwhelmed?*

He remembers a time when the business was new, and he was spread pretty thin. Cold calling, bookkeeping, following up on late payments—he used to do it all, in addition to his primary work. All of this drove him to his limits.

By reflecting on this, Ray finds something within himself that allows him to connect with Vera's feeling of complete inundation. In doing so, he no longer sees her as a complainer. Now, he sees someone who wants to do her job well, but who desperately needs help.

This, in turn, moves Ray to show compassionate empathy, by finding ways to give Vera the help that she needs. He might ask her directly if she has any suggestions that would ease the situation. Maybe he can spread some of the workload to other members of the team. He could even offer that she take a day off to recharge. In addition to benefiting from her employer's suggestions, Vera is encouraged by his sincere efforts to help, which gives her added motivation and inspires her to give her best.

Of course, not every employer or manager will have the resources or circumstances to help in these ways. But when you work to connect with others' feelings, you will be impelled to do what you can.

Emotional empathy is so valuable in everyday life because it allows you to extend beyond shared circumstances. It can help you understand people from various backgrounds and cultures or help you connect with those suffering from a sickness or disability you've never experienced.

So, how can you develop emotional empathy?

➤ **TRY THIS:** When a person tells you about a personal struggle, listen carefully. Resist the urge to judge the person or situation, to interrupt and share your personal experience, or to propose a solution. Instead, focus on understanding the how and why: how the person feels, and why they feel that way.

Remember that individual experiences vary greatly, as do the emotions that accompany those experiences.

For these reasons, avoid statements like the following:

· I know exactly how you feel.
· I've been through this before.
· I completely understand; or, I get it.

And replace them with statements like the following:

· I'm sorry that happened.
· I can imagine how you may feel.
· Thanks for sharing this. Tell me more.

Sharing emotions isn't easy, so help the person feel secure by thanking them for being open and honest. Depending on the person (and the situation), you may encourage them to express themselves further, using questions such as "How long have you felt this way?" or "Have you ever experienced this type of situation before?" Be careful not to force it, lest the other person feel interrogated.

Most of all, reassure them—through words *and* actions— that you're on their side.

Next, it's important to take time to reflect. Once you have a better understanding of how the person feels, you must find a way to relate.

> **TRY THIS:** Ask yourself: *When have I felt similar to what this person has described?*

Friend and colleague Dr. Hendrie Weisinger, bestselling author of *Emotional Intelligence at Work*, illustrated it perfectly in a conversation we had:

"If a person says, 'I screwed up a presentation,' I don't think of a time I screwed up a presentation—which I have [done] and thought, no big deal. Rather, I think of a time I did feel

I screwed up, maybe on a test or something else important to me. It is the feeling of when you failed that you want to recall, not the event."

Even if the other person is unwilling (or unable) to share their feelings, your imagination can help you manage your relationship.

For example, think about how your actions or communication style change when you're sick, or under extreme pressure, or dealing with a personal problem. How easy are you to deal with in such circumstances? Remembering that the other person may be feeling similarly can help you exercise patience and make the best of difficult circumstances.

Of course, you'll never be able to imagine *exactly* how another person feels. But trying will get you a lot closer than you would be otherwise.

Once you find a way to connect with the other person's feelings, and have a more complete picture of the situation, you're ready to show compassionate empathy. In this step, you take action to help however you can.

> **TRY THIS:** Begin by asking the other person directly what you can do to help. If they are unable (or unwilling) to share, ask yourself: *What helped me when I felt similarly?* Or: *What would have helped me?*

It's fine to share your experience or make suggestions, but avoid conveying the impression that you've seen it all or have all the answers. Instead, relate it as something that has helped you in the past. Present it as an option that can be adapted to their circumstances, instead of an all-inclusive solution.

Remember that what worked for you, or even others, may not work for this person. But don't let that hold you back from helping. Simply do what you can.

The downsides of empathy

Along with the many benefits that come with showing empathy, it's important to also acknowledge its limitations and dangers. Since empathy draws from our emotional experience, and powerful emotions are often short-lived, completely relying on empathy for decision-making can prove disastrous.

Paul Bloom is a psychologist and professor at Yale University and the author of the book *Against Empathy*. Bloom argues that empathy has the tendency to blind people to the long-term consequences of their actions. This can be seen in the way governments use empathic engagement—the tendency for people to get caught up in the suffering of victims—to convince their constituents of the need to go to war. But there is rarely mention of the countless lives that will be lost in that war or how many new problems the war will create.

Consider another way empathy could harm rather than help. You may sincerely feel another person's pain in your heart, but if you aren't ready or willing to help the person in the way they truly need, you might resort to a "quick fix" or "easy out." And while those actions may assuage your own feelings of hurt, they don't really solve the problem; in fact, they could make things worse.

For example, consider the experience of my friend Nicole, on her first trip to India.

As Nicole walked the streets, she admired the beautiful architecture and fell in love with the kind and smiling people. But she also couldn't help but feel sharp, emotional pain as she observed so many living in poverty.

Suddenly, a little boy approached her with an open hand. Moved to pity, she gave the child a few coins.

Out of nowhere, an older man appeared, yelling hysterically and waving a large staff, directing insults at my friend. Nicole immediately jumped away in fear, practically running away from the man. Once she was at a safe distance, she asked why the man was so upset.

"He said you shouldn't have given that little boy any money," someone else translated. "The boy is smart, young, and strong, and could work hard to build a good life for himself. But you're robbing him of that—by teaching him to live off handouts."

Nicole was deeply affected by this experience. She had been motivated by empathy: she simply wanted to help, and she thought if she were in the boy's position she would be grateful for a small donation. But after more reflection, she wondered if the man was right. Was she actually contributing to the problem?

There's another potential downside to sharing the thoughts and feelings of others—doing so is emotionally draining. Dr. Robin Stern and Dr. Diana Divecha, researchers who work with the Yale Center for Emotional Intelligence, describe this as "the empathy trap."

"The art of empathy requires paying attention to another's needs without sacrificing one's own," they write. "What turns empathy into a true high-wire act is that its beneficiaries find the attention deeply rewarding... To put ourselves in someone else's shoes, we must strike a balance between emotion and thought and between self and other. Otherwise, empathy becomes a trap, and we can feel as if we're being held hostage by the feelings of others."

Failure to recognize this fact can easily lead to physical and psychological exhaustion.

For example, numerous studies have found that nurses who work with terminally ill patients are at an especially high risk of developing compassion fatigue, defined as "a combination of physical, emotional, and spiritual depletion associated with caring for patients in significant emotional pain and physical distress." The temptation is for caregivers to pay more attention to patients' needs than to their own, which essentially puts them on a path to burnout.

Of course, you don't have to be a nurse or caregiver to fall into the empathy trap. For example, the Pew Research Center analyzed a series of studies and found that in certain cases, the use of social media led to higher levels of stress. Why? Essentially, because users were made more aware of the struggles of those in their network.

For example:

- If a woman was aware that someone close to them experienced the death of a child, partner, or spouse, she scored 14 percent higher on her own measure of stress.
- If a woman was aware that an acquaintance experienced a demotion or cut in pay, she reported 9 percent higher levels of psychological stress.
- If a woman was aware that someone close to her was hospitalized or experienced a serious accident or injury, she reported 5 percent higher psychological stress.

The problem isn't that social media users become aware of negative events in the lives of others. Rather, it's that the rise in digital technology allows individuals to learn about these things much more quickly, and in closer succession. True, becoming informed about such events offers an individual more chances to provide support and comfort. But constant exposure to the problems of others could lead to emotional exhaustion.

As useful as empathy can be to fostering connection and building relationships, it can clearly be harmful in certain contexts.

So, how can you keep empathy in its place?

Emotionally intelligent empathy

The key to emotionally intelligent empathy—that is, making empathy work for you, instead of against you—is to find the right balance.

First and foremost, remember that the goal of empathy is to help you better understand others and their emotional needs—but not at the expense of your own. If you've ever been on an airplane, you know the rule: secure your own oxygen mask before attempting to help others. Otherwise, you won't be helping very much... or for very long. Similarly, to show empathy properly it's helpful to understand your own emotions and needs first. That includes building self-awareness; for example, through the exercises introduced in earlier chapters of this book.

One challenge is that emotional empathy isn't really a quality you can turn off and on. Once you've developed the ability to tune into the feelings of others, you experience it automatically. (You may notice this when you are suddenly moved to tears when hearing a story, watching a film, or listening to a song.) The goal is to show empathy without burning yourself out, and that requires setting limits or even removing yourself from certain situations.

➤ **TRY THIS:** If your job requires you to remain "on" for long periods of time (e.g., a teacher or nurse), it's easy to reach emotional exhaustion. To avoid that outcome, you may decide to take shorter but more frequent breaks to allow yourself to recharge. Or, you may work together with your employer or colleagues to reallocate certain tasks or duties (or at least when those tasks and duties are performed), leading to a more balanced workday for everyone.

➤ **TRY THIS:** Let's say your spouse comes home after a bad day at work. But you had a horrible day, too. You feel in no shape to offer comfort or empathy; in fact, you're craving it yourself.

In this situation, you might say something like: "I'm so sorry to hear you had a tough day; mine was really bad, too. Can we just take some time to relax (or exercise, or enjoy a meal together)? Maybe later we can go for a walk and talk about it all."

This type of response clearly states your own needs while kindly addressing the needs of your partner. And while it only takes a few seconds to say, it can greatly affect how the next few hours, or even days, play out.

➤ **TRY THIS:** If you find that social media is draining your emotional power, set limits regarding how long you will spend on it. Set an alarm and plan something for when your time is up so that you're motivated to shut off your device.

Finally, emotionally intelligent empathy also includes recognizing when someone doesn't want your help or simply isn't ready to share their thoughts or feelings. In these cases, give the person as much time or space as you can. Let them know you're available to talk if and when they need it, and don't be afraid to check back in with them after you let some time pass.

Empathy in action

Facebook executive Sheryl Sandberg recently demonstrated a real-life example of compassionate empathy.

Sandberg had been dealing with the tragedy of losing her husband, who passed away unexpectedly on a trip to Mexico in 2015. Suddenly, she had to deal not only with the emotional pain of losing a spouse, but also the challenge of raising her two children alone. Just a month after her husband's passing, Sandberg gave us a window into her thoughts and emotions via an update she posted on Facebook.

"I think when tragedy occurs, it presents a choice," she wrote. "You can give in to the void, the emptiness that fills your heart, your lungs, constricts your ability to think or even breathe. Or you can try to find meaning."

With that post, Sandberg revealed a glimpse of her extraordinary grief. But she also showed that she wanted to learn from her newfound circumstances and somehow use those learnings to help others.

In February 2017, Sandberg wrote another Facebook post—this time to announce significant changes to her company's policies, which included varying amounts of paid leave to grieve immediate and extended family members, as well as to care for family members or relatives who were suffering from short- or long-term illnesses.

"Amid the nightmare of Dave's death when my kids needed me more than ever, I was grateful every day to work for a company that provides bereavement leave and flexibility," wrote Sandberg. "I needed both to start my recovery."

Sandberg did more than simply find a way to move on. She used her misfortune as a catalyst to reflect on how others might be affected by similar circumstances. And beyond allowing herself to just feel empathy, she *exercised* it: by taking steps to help others.

Of course, you don't have to be an executive to show compassionate empathy to others; the opportunities are there every day.

The next time your spouse, colleague, friend, or family member tells you they're feeling run-down, don't view this in a negative light; instead, remember how they (or someone else) helped you the last time you felt similarly. Then, use that example to do something positive to lift them up.

This is what compassionate empathy is all about: the ability to transform perspective-taking and compassion into positive action. It's about showing others that even if you don't understand exactly what they're going through, you see they're in pain, and you want to help.

Showing empathy in this way takes time and effort, but it's an investment that builds strong connections and brings out the best in others.

Worth its weight in gold

Empathy is an essential component of emotional intelligence, one that fuels the connection between you and others. It requires a combination of skills, including good listening and active use of the imagination.

At its core, the concept of empathy is well summed up in the maxim known as "the Golden Rule": treat others the way you want to be treated.

In a few simple words, the Golden Rule embodies all three elements of empathy: cognitive, emotional, and compassionate. To follow it, one must not only think and feel, but take positive action as well.

Critics claim the Golden Rule is broken. After all, individual values and tastes differ. Shouldn't it be: "Treat others as *they* want to be treated"?

But this reasoning misses the point; the beauty of this principle is in its practicality. The Golden Rule is easy to remember, while encouraging consideration and connection. Further, to fulfill the Golden Rule in the ultimate sense *requires* taking others' tastes, values, and perspectives into consideration.

After all, isn't that what you'd want them to do when dealing with you?

Make no mistake, though: living by this rule isn't easy. It means resisting the urge to jump to conclusions—something we love to do—and instead giving others the benefit of the doubt. But when used in an emotionally intelligent way, empathy can vastly improve the quality of your relationships—and even the quality of your life.

Remember Mr. Pierce, the executive from my opening story?

Sadly, he passed away a few years ago. I've often wondered how many similar emails, letters, and requests he read over the years. A press release made the following statement:

"Mr. Pierce served on various committees... [and] his organizational responsibilities required that he travel extensively... Despite his workload, he was well known for never being too busy to listen to those needing assistance or advice, and he put others at ease with his warm smile and good sense of humor. His closest associates noted that people from different backgrounds or cultures were naturally drawn to him."

I never forgot the lessons Mr. Pierce taught me so long ago. And I'm sure countless others haven't forgotten either.

Empathy is invaluable. It makes us more flexible, understanding, and a joy to be around. But while the ability to share the feelings of others is a gift, it is one that must be harnessed—lest it cause harm.

Learn to do that and not only will you strengthen your relationships, you will also enrich your personal life—as you learn to experience the world through the eyes of others.

6

The Power of Influence

How Emotional Connection Breaks Down Barriers and Changes Minds

· · · · ·

Those that will not hear must be made to feel.

GERMAN PROVERB

CHRIS VOSS MAY be the best negotiator in the world. Voss spent more than two decades in the FBI, including fifteen years as a hostage negotiator, during which he worked on more than 150 international hostage cases. Eventually, he was chosen among thousands of agents to serve as the FBI's lead international kidnapping negotiator—a position he held for four years.

Voss recalls one day in 1998, standing in a narrow hallway outside an apartment in Harlem, New York City. Three heavily armed fugitives were reportedly inside, the same fugitives who had engaged in a shoot-out with rival gang members some days before. A SWAT team stood at attention just a few steps behind Voss. Voss's job: convince the fugitives to give up without a fight.

With no telephone number to call, Voss was forced to speak through the apartment door. He did so for six hours, with no response. He began to question if anyone was even inside.

Suddenly, the door opened. A woman walked out, followed by all three fugitives.

Not a single shot fired. No loss of life. Not even a harsh word.

How did he do it?

Using what he describes as his "late-night FM DJ voice," Voss repeated variations of the following: "It looks like you don't want to come out. It seems like you worry that if you open the door, we'll come in with guns blazing. It looks like you don't want to go back to jail."

Afterwards, Voss was curious as to what specifically convinced the fugitives to finally come out.

"We didn't want to get caught or get shot, but you calmed us down," they said. "We finally believed you wouldn't go away, so we just came out."

Over the years, Voss fine-tuned his negotiation methods, allowing him to save hundreds of lives.

"It's not me bringing emotion in; it's already there," Voss told me in an interview. "It's the elephant in the room. There's this monstrous creature in the middle of every communication: it's what we want and it's based on what we care about. Each one of us, we make every single decision based on what we care about and that makes decision-making, by definition, an emotional process.

"My approach is, let's stop kidding ourselves. Hostage negotiators don't kid themselves about emotions. It's all about navigating emotions, and one step leads to another, which then puts you in a position to influence others. It's based on trust and it allows you to influence outcomes.

"It allows you to change people's minds."

The world is your training field

You may never deal with a hostage situation, but every day you are faced with countless opportunities to influence and be influenced.

With each interaction with another person, a relationship is created or affected. Some of these relationships are short-lived, like a salesperson you meet and never see again. Other relationships—like those with family and friends—will last a lifetime. But every connection with another person involves both an exchange and an opportunity: to help or be helped, to harm or be harmed.

Relationship management is about making the most of these interactions. It is founded on the principle of influence—your capacity to affect others and their behavior, and their ability to affect you. But while some influence occurs naturally and unintentionally—the more time you spend with someone, the greater influence you exert on them, and vice versa—managing relationships is done with purpose. It includes using the other three skills of emotional intelligence—self-awareness, self-management, and social awareness—to help you persuade and motivate others, to more effectively manage conflict, and to maximize benefits.

In this chapter, we'll examine the nuances of influence and see what managing relationships looks like in the real world—and how it can help you be a better partner in all areas of life.

The goal is simple: to get the best out of others and allow them to get the best out of you.

Defining influence

Influence is the act of affecting a person's character or behavior by means other than force or direct command. It is often unnoticeable: an American who moves to the UK may not realize the influence her new peers have on her vocabulary and accent—until she returns home and her family tells her how different she sounds.

A person could also unintentionally influence in negative ways. A young man who lacks social awareness might not realize he has a tendency to talk about himself too much—so much so that others avoid him when possible. A close friend might be so pushy with their opinions that you quit asking for them. Both are totally oblivious to how they're perceived by others.

Then there's *intentional* influence. Influencers use the principles of persuasion and motivation to overcome obstacles or manage conflict. They inspire others to think differently, to see things from a new perspective, and even to change their behavior.

Such attempts at influence can be short-term. For example, you might try to:

- Persuade your significant other of the need to buy something (or not buy something).
- Incline your child to clean their room, without asking them directly to do so.
- Calm down a friend who's upset.

Or, you may attempt to influence someone over a longer period of time, such as when you try to:

- Help your spouse quit smoking or get more exercise.
- Keep your boss from micromanaging you.
- Instill character and personal values into your children.

Of course, the ability to influence is a tool that can be used to harm just as it can be used to help. In chapter eight, we'll consider how influence and other traits of emotional intelligence can be used for unsavory purposes—as well as how you can protect yourself.

But first let's take a close look at various methods of influence to see how they work in the real world.

Show personal interest

In the classic book *How to Win Friends and Influence People*, Dale Carnegie relates the time he met a distinguished botanist at a dinner party.

Throughout the evening, Carnegie writes, he sat at the edge of his chair, fascinated by the man's stories of exotic plants and garden experiments. Carnegie kept him engaged with questions about his own gardening problems and expressed appreciation for his help. When it came time to leave, the botanist turned to the host of the dinner party and praised Carnegie as "most stimulating" and a "most interesting conversationalist."

This story marvelously illustrates one of the first keys to influence: showing personal interest.

When you treat others as interesting, you ask questions— not in an invasive or nosy way, but out of curiosity. Where are you from? Where did you grow up? Where have you been? Those are three variations of one simple question that could lead to hours of potential conversation.

"If you aspire to be a good conversationalist," advised Carnegie, "be an attentive listener.... Remember that the people you are talking to are a hundred times more interested in themselves and their wants and problems than they are in you and your problems."

Carnegie's advice was valuable when he penned it, but it's even more relevant today because the rise of modern technology has reduced most attention spans. Go to any restaurant, and you'll be sure to find a few individuals who can't resist the urge to check their phones every few minutes, often to the chagrin of their dinner partners.

In contrast, when you treat your conversation partner as the most interesting person in the room—being curious to hear their thoughts and opinions—you stand out as different. There's no right or wrong in this conversation; it's simply perspective-taking. When you endeavor to understand why another person thinks and feels the way they do, they become naturally intrigued about you. As a by-product, they are more open to hear and consider your thoughts and opinions—even if they disagree with them.

Treating others as interesting keeps them at the forefront, and, ironically, makes you the person everyone loves to be around. Because who doesn't enjoy talking about themselves?

Encourage respect

Respect begets respect. For some, this may seem like common sense. But as a society the ability to show respect is becoming a lost art. Sarcasm and cutting remarks have become the default reaction, at work and home. Further, when we get caught up in emotion it's easy to forget the principles of common courtesy.

Here are a few tips that can help you earn others' respect.

1. Acknowledge others.
Even before you say a word to someone, you can show respect by acknowledging the person's presence. A slight nod of the head, a smile, or a simple hello can go a long way in making a first impression.

When discussing a topic on which you disagree, learn to acknowledge your partner's points. Thank them for being open and sharing their perspective. If you don't follow their reasoning, ask follow-up questions. To clarify, try rephrasing their points in your own words, and ask if you've got it right. All of these practices help others feel heard.

2. Get the full story.

Be careful about jumping to conclusions based on events or situations you didn't witness firsthand. In such cases, there's a big chance that details and context have been lost in the mix. And even if you witnessed a situation firsthand, you did so through a lens of personal biases and leanings that affect your perception.

Be careful to get the details of a situation before taking action. Ask others involved to describe how they remember things going down. Others will appreciate the time you take to get their side of the story, which promotes respectful discussion.

3. Set the tone.

If you approach people in a calm and reasonable manner, chances are much higher that they will respond in the same way. Acknowledge their difficulties and challenges and they'll be much more willing to listen. In contrast, if you begin with biting sarcasm, or by yelling, you'll send the other person's amygdala into overdrive.

If you're trying to get a point across, aim to be kind and fair, not accusatory. The old saying is true: you'll catch more flies with honey than with vinegar. At the very least, make honey the appetizer.

4. Keep a balanced view of yourself.

People quickly lose respect for those who appear arrogant or conceited. But the other extreme is also dangerous: if you lack conviction or confidence, you'll appear weak and be labeled a pushover.

Instead, strive to achieve a balanced view of yourself in relation to others. You have plenty of value to offer, but so do they. Maintaining this view isn't always easy, especially when you encounter an opinion or belief system that differs sharply from your own. But it's possible if you focus on identifying strengths—both your own and those of the people you're dealing with.

Reason with empathy

You're having a conversation that suddenly turns to a controversial subject you happen to feel strongly about. Your conversation partner holds the opposite opinion and begins to express their beliefs in strong terms.

How do you respond?

In many cases, you may not wish to continue speaking at all. You may decide that it's not worth the emotional investment or that it's not the right time or place. Or, you may jump in with little regard for the other perspective, vehemently attacking the other person as "wrong," while trying to prove your points with arguments that appeal to your own set of (often-unshared) values. You may even resort to attacking the other person's character, accusing them of lacking common sense or decency. This attack provokes a like-minded emotional response. The ensuing back-and-forth accomplishes nothing, only an end result where both you and your adversary have dug in your heels and are further apart than when you began.

There is, however, a better way. It's called reasoning with empathy.

An approach based on reason is sound, fair, and sensible. The problem is, what one person considers sound, fair, and sensible is much different from someone else's assessment—especially when dealing with controversial topics. That's why empathy is so important: it allows you to reason from the other person's point of view instead of your own.

Reasoning with empathy promotes active listening and gives others something to think about, long after the conversation is over. It helps pave the way for future discussion, increasing the possibility that a person considers an alternative point of view or even changes their mind.

So, instead of turning people off with your arguments, how can you get them to listen and think?

1. Begin with common ground.

When attempting to persuade or convince, it's important to first find something upon which you both agree. It helps to view your counterpart as a partner or ally instead of an enemy.

"Effective persuaders must be adept at describing their positions in terms that illuminate their advantages," explains esteemed business professor Jay Conger, author of *The Necessary Art of Persuasion*. "As any parent can tell you, the fastest way to get a child to come along willingly on a trip to the grocery store is to point out there are lollipops by the cash register… In [other] situations, persuasive framing is obviously more complex, but the underlying principle is the same. It is a process of identifying shared benefits."

When choosing how to frame your reasoning it's critical that you first understand your audience. Of course, you need to know which issues are important to them, but it's just as vital that you understand why those issues are important. If you fail here, your efforts to convince may be misdirected.

Therefore, finding a common ground means doing some homework: conversing with your audience and those close to them and listening closely to their input.

"Those steps help [the best persuaders] think through the arguments, the evidence, and the perspectives they will present," explains Conger. "Oftentimes, this process causes them to alter or compromise their own plans before they even start persuading. It is through this thoughtful, inquisitive approach they develop frames that appeal to their audience."

To illustrate, let's say you're trying to convince your supervisor to give you a raise. You could go in with guns blazing, detailing your longtime service to the company, your special skill set, and your long list of accomplishments. In your mind, this is an extremely convincing argument.

Unbeknownst to you, however, your supervisor is under fire for being over budget and is willing to do anything to solve this problem—even downsize the team. Sensing your dissatisfaction with the current situation, they may decide the easiest option is to cut you.

But what if you focused first on getting to know your supervisor's needs? By doing your research, you find out their current priorities. You understand that if you can help them get the department under budget, you're in a much better position to ask for a raise.

This empathetic approach helps you frame your reasoning around your supervisor's priorities, provide a concrete solution to their most important problem, and increase the chance of getting what you want as well.

2. Ask strategic questions.

It's important to continue learning about your counterpart, even once you're in the thick of the discussion.

Asking the right questions will give your partner the opportunity to express themselves and reveal their thinking on the topic at hand, encouraging a more open discussion and allowing you to better understand their position.

For example:

- What are your feelings toward... ?
- What convinced you that... ?
- How would you react if... ?
- What would change your feelings on... ?

Additionally, asking someone for a step-by-step explanation of their beliefs can encourage them to think more deeply about a matter. Often, they'll realize they don't understand the issue as well as they thought, leading them to soften their position.

3. Provide evidence that your partner is likely to respect.

Any argument requires proof to be convincing. But in a world that is full of misleading data and outright false information, how can you find evidence that is both persuasive and accurate?

Remember that people differ in background, upbringing, and culture—what one person finds convincing may not work for another. That's why you must closely examine the arguments of your conversation partner. Who influences and inspires them? What research or sources do they cite? After answering these questions, you can seek data and expert opinions from sources they are likely to respect. (Be careful not to misquote or take information out of context, which will erode your credibility.)

To be sure, these efforts are time-consuming and challenging. But it's a well-spent investment, because it allows you to present evidence in a way that's more appealing to your partner instead of wasting time on arguments they're never likely to consider.

4. Know when to yield.

In the course of a discussion, you may become even more convinced that the other person is wrong. You may see key weaknesses in their position and be tempted to "go for the kill."

But people are emotionally attached to their beliefs. If you mercilessly expose every flaw in your partner's reasoning, they'll feel attacked. The amygdala will take over, and their focus will no longer be on listening or reasonable discussion; rather, they will defend themselves or attack in return.

Instead of attempting to exercise dominance, focus on learning more about the other person's viewpoint, as well as the reasons behind their feelings. Then, focus on re-establishing common ground, with the goal of laying a foundation you can build upon later. Above all, strive to leave the conversation on a positive note—by thanking the person for openly expressing their opinion and for helping you understand their point of view.

Remember that lasting influence takes time. Your goal isn't to "win the argument" or change someone's mind in a single discussion. Rather, strive to see the bigger picture.

Tact is the knack of making a point without making an enemy.

ISAAC NEWTON

Stir their emotions

Convincing someone of a truth is very different from motivating them to do something about it.

In order to truly galvanize others to action, you have to stir their emotions—penetrating deeply to affect a person's thoughts and feelings.

Artists are experts at eliciting an emotional response. Think about your favorite actor, dancer, or musician. Most likely, these artists appeal to you because of their ability to make you feel. Despite you never having met these individuals, they are able to reach you on an intimate level. They get you to laugh, to cry, to dance when nobody's looking.

Or think back to your school days. Can you remember your favorite teacher or professor? They had that remarkable ability to bring dry facts to life. The stories they told, the personal interest they showed—seeing them was the highlight of your day. Possibly, that teacher played a profound role in shaping the person you are today.

Although the context in which you seek influence is different, the principles of making emotional connections are the same. To have any chance of motivating others to action, you have to stir their emotions.

Here are a few ways to do it.

1. Show passion.

Enthusiasm is contagious. If you truly believe in what you have to say, your passion will come across naturally and can inspire others. (Think of the infectious energy of a good coach or personal trainer.)

This doesn't mean that you have to put on a show or be something you're not. Of primary importance is that *you're* thoroughly convinced. If you're not, take time to ponder your idea or beliefs, to think things through. Focus on adding value. Then your passion will be authentic.

2. Use illustrations and the power of storytelling.

Numbers, data, and a well-crafted argument are important aspects of convincing evidence. But used alone, their reach is extremely limited. Simply put, they're boring.

But everyone loves a great story. When you can use an anecdote or factual example to illustrate your topic, you bring it to life for your listener. It engages their mental faculties; it touches them. You also bridge the link between theory and practice.

Don't just recount the facts; find a way to bring them to life.

3. Repeat. Repeat. Repeat.

The greatest teachers are masters of repetition. Just think of how many times your parents had to tell you the same thing before you really got it. Or pay attention to how great orators periodically repeat a key phrase, almost like the hook or chorus to your favorite song. Martin Luther King Jr.'s masterful use of that single phrase "I have a dream" is a great example.

And then there's the classic presentation advice: Tell your audience what you're going to tell them. Then tell them. Then tell them what you told them.

Mastering the art of repetition can be challenging, lest you appear stiff or rigid. But while repetition of a key phrase can be powerful, you can also reframe your main points by using expressions like the following:

- In other words (or, In essence)...
- What I'm trying to say is...
- Here's the point (or, Here's the takeaway)...

This technique allows you to repeat key points while maintaining variety and puts you in control of what your listeners are most likely to remember.

4. Use the element of surprise.

An unorthodox or "shocking" statement can really grab someone's attention. For example, writer friend Lyz Lenz once penned a brilliant piece that led with the headline: "Dear Daughter, I Want You to Fail."

The article is all about how Lenz learned to deal with failure at an early age, to learn from mistakes and bounce back stronger than ever. She contrasts that with a trend in which so-called "snowplow parents" attempt to consistently guard their children from failure, to smooth their path and make life easier.

"A life lived without failure is not success, it's mediocrity," argues Lenz. "I don't want to teach my daughter to quit or that I will pave her way. I want to teach her to pull back, reformulate and try again and again and again."

Great reasoning, and excellent points. But without that powerful hook, the majority of the audience would never have read the article. You can do the same. By using a startling statement to reel your listener in emotionally, you get them to pay attention. Then, deliver a message that reinforces your common values.

On the Home Front

Let's say you're calmly discussing a matter with a romantic partner. Before long, you reach a major disagreement, and you notice that your partner is becoming highly emotional. You could continue arguing your point and risk the other person losing control. Or you could allow your partner to speak their mind, listen carefully, and then try to find a way to move on.

By helping your partner calm down, you influence their emotions. But then what? If the subject is an important one, you'll need to revisit it in a future discussion. How can you do so effectively?

Give careful thought to the ideal location and time to speak. For example, choose a time when both of you are relaxed and in a positive mood. You should also consider how you will reintroduce the subject. Remember that opening with an apology (if appropriate), with an expression of thanks, or with some common ground will promote a more positive atmosphere and increase the opportunity for understanding and cooperation.

Influence in action: Compassion on the big stage

For Celine Dion, one of the most recognized and celebrated singers on the planet, it was just another day at work. She was performing in front of a crowd of thousands, as she had done countless times before, this time at Caesars Palace in Las Vegas. Suddenly, a fan who appeared to be intoxicated rushed the stage, managing to get right next to Dion. The fan then resisted the security guards' attempts to remove her.

This situation could have quickly turned ugly, if not for Dion's remarkable poise and handling of the moment.

Instead of deferring to her bodyguards or simply running away, Dion showed respect to the fan by acknowledging her and speaking to her. Dion even expressed appreciation for the fan.

"Let me tell you something," said Dion as she clasped the woman's hand. "I'm glad you came up on stage tonight. I'm glad that . . . you just wanted to come closer to me."

At this point, the fan grabbed the singer and wrapped her leg around her. The guards immediately drew closer, but Dion held them at bay for the moment, asking them to stay close by in case she needed help. She then continued to speak to the woman in a calm, soothing voice.

The fan then said something inaudible to the audience, but Dion heard something that she used to strike a common ground and form a connection. "You know what?" Dion said. "We got something in common. We got babies that we love. And we're going to fight for them. And we're [both] wearing gold. That's a sign."

Throughout the experience, Dion demonstrated striking empathy. By encouraging her to sing and dance, Dion changed the woman's mood from rebellious and combative to joyful and cooperative. And in under two minutes, Dion convinced the disrupter to walk offstage with her "friends" (the guards), making the absolute best of a challenging situation.

Afterwards, Dion fell to the stage in relief, to wild applause from the crowd.

That's emotional influence at its finest.

Reaching others

Whether it's interviewing for a job, looking for a discount, or asking someone out on a date, all of us try to influence at one point or another.

But remember that the process of influence is a progression.

When I spoke to Chris Voss, whose story began this chapter, he likened this process to a stairway. "The tendency is to go directly at what you want," he explained. "But in this case, the shortest distance between two points is *not* a straight line. It involves taking steps, and each step becomes the foundation for the next. It's about building rapport—and that requires empathy. And one step leads to another, which then puts you in a position to influence others."

In order to convince someone to think differently, you must first understand how they think. Get to know their pain points so you can help solve them. Learn their communication style, along with their personal drivers and motivations. This will allow you to speak in a way they understand.

Even more importantly, this will help you reach them emotionally—which will in turn motivate them to act.

But you must also realize that people and situations are constantly changing. Your most important relationships are molded through years of interactions.

So, how can emotional intelligence help you enjoy higher-quality relationships?

It requires building on a solid foundation—and that's the subject of our next chapter.

7

Building Bridges

Cultivating Deeper, Healthier, More Loyal Relationships

● ● ● ● ●

No man is an island.

JOHN DONNE

OVER THE PAST decade, I've met or interviewed countless executives, managers, and entrepreneurs. Many
of these people built careers and businesses based
on blood, sweat, and tears... but when it comes to work
ethic, not one of them could hold a candle to my mother-in-
law, Margret.

Margret ("Mom" to me) was born in Poland in 1958, in
hard times. She knew what it was like to struggle, so she never
took anything for granted. She taught her two daughters to do
the same—to enjoy the good times, prepare for the hard times,
and cultivate strong relationships.

This last one came naturally to Mom. From those whom she had just met to others who knew her for years, everyone sensed that Mom cared—and this drew them to her. For example, when she decided to leave a job cleaning the office of an executive at a major car manufacturer, his secretary begged her to stay. She trusted Mom immensely and had grown accustomed to their refreshing chats. Mom still decided to move on, but she had left a lasting impression. That secretary never lost contact, periodically stopping by Mom's home to catch up over a cup of coffee.

Or how about Laurie and Verdis, the couple Mom made friends with on one family vacation to Hawaii. Laurie had been introduced as a friend of a friend, but she and Mom quickly became close. They were soon inseparable, and when the vacation was over, both were in tears as they said good-bye. Mom and Laurie stayed in regular contact over the years, mostly through letters and emails. None of that may sound extraordinary, except for one small detail...

Mom didn't speak English. She and Laurie communicated through translators (usually my wife). Yet somehow they managed to form an unbreakable bond.

Even in her final hours, Mom was still making friends. She wouldn't stop thanking the doctors and nurses working at her hospital station, and she wanted to introduce all of us when we went to visit. Mom was amazed at their ability to remain positive, kind, and compassionate despite the nature of their job, which had them seeing pain and suffering every day. They deserved recognition and appreciation. Mom helped give it to them.

I could go on about Mom's ability to connect with others—the years she spent caring for her own aged mother and mother-in-law, the endless hours volunteering her time to help others. But of all the lessons Mom taught me through

the years, this was the greatest: Cultivating meaningful relationships is hard work. But it's more than worth the effort.

The value of strong relationships

Our lives depend on our relationships with others. From the
moment we're born, we rely on others to help raise us, nur-
ture us, care for us. No matter how independent or self-reliant
we become, we will always accomplish more with the help
of others.

But achievements are only the beginning. Research
indicates that good relationships also make us happier and
healthier.*

So, how can you cultivate better relationships?

A few years ago, a research team at Google set out on
a quest to figure out what makes teams successful. They
code-named the study Project Aristotle, a tribute to the philosopher's famous quote: "The whole is greater than the sum
of its parts."

The research team analyzed dozens of teams and interviewed hundreds of executives, team leads, and team members.
They found that a number of elements contributed to a
team's effectiveness—but the single greatest factor was that
team members felt something called "psychological safety."

"In a team with high psychological safety, teammates feel
safe to take risks around their team members," wrote the
researchers. "They feel confident that no one on the team

---

* Robert Waldinger is a psychiatrist and is currently directing the Harvard Study of Adult
Development, one of the most comprehensive studies of emotional well-being in history.
When asked to present his conclusions of this seventy-five-year study, he cited the following as the message that came through loud and clear: "Good relationships keep us happier
and healthier. Period."

will embarrass or punish anyone else for admitting a mistake, asking a question, or offering a new idea."

Simply put, great teams thrive on trust.

At times, we hand over trust to complete strangers without a second thought—the pilot tasked to fly us home or the chef who cooks our food when we go out to eat. But this type of trust is circumstantial; it comes and goes depending on the situation. To build trust into deeper relationships requires providing others with benefits over a longer period of time.

We might imagine each of our relationships as a bridge we build between us and another person. Any strong bridge must be built on a solid foundation—and for relationships, that foundation is trust. Without trust, there can be no love, no friendship, no lasting connection between people. But where there is trust, there is motivation to act. If you trust someone is looking after your best interests, you will do almost anything that person asks of you.

In this chapter, I'll outline practical tips you can follow to truly earn the trust of others. As you read, reflect on the people in your life. How do the ones you trust practice these behaviors? In what areas can you personally improve?

Answering those questions will help you to both cultivate and maintain deeper, more meaningful relationships.

Communication

Building trust requires communication that's both effective *and* consistent.

Consistent communication allows you to stay in touch with another person's reality. You become quickly aware of their highs and lows, and how they deal with them. Further, you send the message that what's important to them is important to you.

For example, one series of recent studies led research organization Gallup to conclude that the most effective managers use a combination of face-to-face, phone, and electronic communication to reach employees, and they return calls or messages within twenty-four hours. Additionally, Gallup found that most employees value communication from their managers about "what happens in their lives outside of work." All of this contributes to the feeling that the manager or team lead is invested in the employee as a real person.

Since individuals have different ways of thinking and different communication styles, it's also important that you express yourself clearly. Remember that no one can read your mind. Some individuals need more detail than others, so work to express yourself in a way that others can understand.

How about at home? It isn't easy to find time to communicate. Parents work longer hours than ever. Children spend most of their day at school or with friends, and when they are at home they're probably glued to their phones or computers. How can you achieve more consistent communication with your loved ones?

> **TRY THIS:** Set a goal to eat one meal together per day. And instead of competing with electronic devices, take advantage of them—use electronic messaging or social media as a way to keep in contact with family members. Share part of your day, then ask them about theirs. This isn't meant to replace face-to-face communication; rather, you want to supplement it. Sending a short message to your spouse or children, just to say "thank you," "thinking of you," or "love you," can help build feelings of trust and emotional security—and increase the desire to spend more personal time together.

Authenticity

Authenticity fosters trust. We are drawn to the people we feel are genuine, the ones who "keep it real." But what does it truly mean to be authentic?

Authentic people share their true thoughts and feelings with others. They know not everyone will agree with them, and they realize this is okay. They also understand that they aren't perfect, but they're willing to show those imperfections because they know everyone else has them, too. By accepting others for who they are, authentic individuals prove relatable.

Of course, to "be authentic" is easier said than done. In fact, certain aspects of emotional intelligence can actually get in the way.

For example, if you possess increased social awareness, you're probably sensitive to the impact your words and actions have on others. That sensitivity can be helpful if it inspires more tact and respect. But it can also hurt your ability to inspire trust if it causes you to consistently hide your true feelings or say things you don't mean.

Apple executive Angela Ahrendts spoke to this point in an interview with journalist Rebecca Jarvis. Asked about the worst career advice she ever received, Ahrendts brought up the time she was working at a big corporation and a human resources manager told her that she needed to make changes—like not talking so emotionally with her hands—if she wanted to be considered "CEO material."

So, at the recommendation of the company Ahrendts traveled to Minneapolis to meet with a coach, where she would be filmed and critiqued. "I was supposed to be there for a couple of days and I went for a couple of hours," explains Ahrendts. "By lunchtime the first day I just looked at them and I said, 'I gotta go. I don't want to be somebody that I'm not. I like me and I've been pretty successful so far being me and I was raised in a really big family. And you know, my mom liked me, my friends liked me... I don't care about a title or a position. You know I have to wake up with me every morning and I want to be the best version of myself. I don't want to be this person you're trying to make me so I'm really sorry but I have to go.' So, I left, and literally a month later got the call to become the CEO of Burberry.

"So, I just think that, to thyself be true."

Authenticity doesn't mean sharing everything about yourself, with everyone, all of the time. It *does* mean saying what you mean, meaning what you say, and sticking to your values and principles above all else.

Not everyone will appreciate you. But the ones who matter will.

Helpfulness

One of the quickest ways to gain someone's trust is to help them.

Think about your favorite boss or teacher. Where they graduated from, what kind of degree they have, even their previous accomplishments—none of this is relevant to your relationship. But what about the hours they were willing to take out of their busy schedule to listen or help out? Their readiness to get down in the trenches and work alongside you?

Actions like these inspire trust.

The same principle applies in your family life. It's often the small things that matter: an offer to make a cup of coffee or tea, pitching in with the dishes or other housework, helping carry in groceries from the car.

In fact, a spirit of helpfulness is what actually helped me woo my wife. We had been friends for a year before I asked her out, but she turned me down. I took it hard. She said we could still be friends—something I wasn't sure I was capable of. But I knew she was special and I wasn't ready to let her out of my life completely, so I agreed.

Somehow, we did manage to remain friends. A year later, I could sense her feelings toward me had started to change… so I asked if she'd reconsider.

In 2018, we celebrate our tenth wedding anniversary.

Once we were together, I asked her what changed her mind about me. "You never stopped being kind and helpful," she said. "Other guys, if you weren't interested in them romantically, they would get mean, or blame you, or become some completely different person. But you didn't. You helped me through some difficult times, even after I rejected you. After we were friends for so long, I got to thinking: I know he'd make a great husband for someone. Why not me?"

Remember, whether you're cultivating a relationship with a friend, a romantic partner, or a colleague: trust is about the long game. Help wherever and whenever you can.

Humility

Developing a helpful attitude requires humility. Being humble doesn't mean that you lack self-confidence or that you never stand up for your own opinions or principles. Rather, it involves recognizing that you don't know everything—and being willing to learn from others.

For example, if you're younger or less experienced than colleagues or clients, acknowledge that and keep it in mind. If you demonstrate a willingness to learn, you will display humility and naturally earn respect.

In contrast, if you're older or more experienced, show respect by not quickly dismissing new ideas or techniques. Instead, dignify those you work with by asking for their opinions and perspectives—and actually paying attention when they speak. When both sides recognize that the other side has something valuable to offer, it creates a safe environment that promotes growth.

Humility also means being willing to apologize.

"I'm sorry" can be the two most difficult words to say, but also the most powerful. When you're willing to admit your mistakes, you make a big statement about how you view yourself in relation to others. This naturally draws others closer to you, building trust and loyalty.

Apologizing doesn't always mean you're wrong and the other person is right. It means you value your relationship more than your ego.

Honesty

Most people realize that honesty and trust go hand in hand. But honest communication requires more than saying what you sincerely believe; it means avoiding half-truths and ensuring the information you present is done in a way that will not be misinterpreted. Focusing on technicalities, loopholes, and escape clauses may win you a trial in court, but it won't win you others' trust.

Those who deceive may achieve temporary success, but sooner or later the truth comes out. In contrast, those who are honest stand out. They're more valuable employees, and they contribute to a feeling of security at home. They are the friends whose opinions actually mean something.

Dependability

It's common nowadays for people to break an agreement or commitment when they feel like it. Whether it's plans for the weekend with a friend, a business deal sealed with a handshake, or a promise made to a loved one, many find it easy to go back on their word when following through presents the slightest inconvenience.

There are plenty of reasons why people go back on their agreements, but it often comes down to a simple truth: we tend to live in the moment. If the immediate benefit to saying yes outweighs the discomfort of saying no, most people make the commitment—without seriously considering if and how they can live up to it.

So, what's the key to staying true to your word?

Building self-awareness and self-control can help you avoid making commitments to which you have no intention of sticking. For example, a positive and enthusiastic outlook may cause you to over-promise at work... but once reality catches up, you tend to under-deliver. Identifying this fact, and training yourself to pause and think twice before over-committing, can help you take on less and better adhere to your deadlines.

Researchers have also found that promise-makers are more likely to keep their commitments when those agreements are connected to a sense of ethical responsibility. In other words, these people deliver on what they say because it's "the right thing to do," even if doing so brings along some type of inconvenience or disadvantage.

Of course, there are different degrees of commitment. Bailing on an evening of Netflix with a friend will probably cause less harm than breaking a promise to your child or missing a business deadline others are depending on. And sometimes, truly extenuating circumstances will interfere with your ability to follow through.

But if you make a habit of keeping your word—in things big and small—you'll develop a strong reputation for reliability and trustworthiness.

Show some love

I led a project years ago and Jessica, the most experienced member of my team, was struggling. The problem wasn't her work—she was performing brilliantly—but she felt a bit burnt out. The client we were serving wasn't an easy one, and Jessica said: "I'm no spring chicken anymore, you know. I can't go on like this much longer."

I reassured her that I appreciated her work and that I would give her a break from assignments like this one for a while. We completed the last few days of work without Jessica, as she moved on to another project. Upon wrapping up, we received stellar feedback from the client, and I knew who I wanted to call first.

After I asked Jessica how the rest of the week went, I let her know the good news. I told her it was some of the best feedback we had ever gotten from *any* client, and how much that meant coming from them. I also thanked her specifically for her role on the project and told her I knew things wouldn't have gone as well without her work.

You could "hear" the smile on the other line. She thanked me (twice) for taking the time to call her. She finished by saying: "You don't know how much this phone call means to me. I'd be happy to help out on a similar project in the future."

Wow. What a change.

This story illustrates the value of sincere and authentic praise. This was no empty flattery, designed just to see what more I could get out of Jessica in the future. It was taking a moment to give credit where credit was due—an act that, unfortunately, many people neglect. In fact, it's one of the most common complaints in any dysfunctional relationship: "I just don't feel appreciated."

People have a great need for praise and commendation. The problem is that it's extremely difficult for some individuals to give positive reinforcement or encouragement to others—because they've never received it themselves. But even if you were raised in an extremely critical environment, it's possible to change your mentality by focusing on the following:

1. Be sincere.

Attempts to flatter or compliment superficially will backfire in the long run. You also shouldn't simply view commendation as another task to be checked off the to-do list. Rather, sincere praise is the result of consistently looking for the positive in others.

But what if you struggle to find something to commend someone on? You might be thinking: I can't be authentic and praise everyone, right?

Wrong.

Everyone deserves commendation for something. By learning to identify, recognize, and praise those talents, you bring out the best in them.

This thinking process trains you to see the good in others, and it will inspire you to give spontaneous commendation. After all, if you saw an employee engaging in dangerous behavior, you wouldn't wait too long to correct it, would you? Similarly, you should positively reinforce your employees' good behavior when you see it—to encourage them to continue.

2. Be specific.

There's value in expressing general appreciation to others, but the more specific you can be, the better. Be sure to tell them what you appreciate, and why.

Here's how this might look in the workplace:

"Hi _____, do you have a minute? I wanted to tell you something. I know I don't say it enough, but I really appreciate what you do around here. The way you [*insert: specific action taking care of a project, client, problem*]—it was great. I could really see your [*insert: specific quality*] in action and how much it benefits the company. Keep up the good work."

How would those words make *you* feel?

Of course, you need to personally own whatever encouragement you give. If you do, others will sense your sincerity and be drawn to it.

A caveat: As with everything, balance is necessary. Commend subpar effort, and that's what you'll continue to receive. Further, if you dish out overly exuberant praise for everything, people will stop taking you seriously.

This is rarely a problem in the real world, however. In truth, far more people feel their efforts are undervalued or go unnoticed. That's part of what makes praise so powerful: if you make it a habit to express appreciation to others, they'll do the same for you.

➤ **TRY THIS:** For one month, schedule twenty minutes a week to reflect on what you appreciate about someone important to you. It could be your significant other (or another member of your family), a friend, a business partner, or a colleague—or even a competitor!

Then, take a moment to write them a short note, give them a call, or go see them in person. Tell them specifically how they help you or what you value about them. Don't address any other topics or problems; just show some love.

Better than Pizza

Dan Ariely, a professor of psychology and behavioral economics at Duke University, highlighted the value of praise in an interesting experiment. In his book *Payoff: The Hidden Logic That Shapes Our Motivations*, Ariely recounts a weeklong exercise in which employees working at a semiconductor factory were promised one of three things if they were able to assemble a certain number of chips per day:

- A cash bonus of approximately $30.
- A voucher for a free pizza.
- A complimentary text message of "Well done!" from the boss.

A fourth group, serving as the control, received nothing.

Interestingly, pizza was the top motivator on day one—increasing productivity by 6.7 percent over the control group. This is somewhat surprising considering the cash only motivated a 4.9 percent increase... and actually resulted in a 6.5 percent *drop* in productivity for the week overall.

But even more interesting was what turned out to be the biggest motivator of the week: the compliment.

Now, if the promise of a simple text message from the boss can increase productivity, can you imagine what real, sincere, and authentic praise would do?

From negative to constructive

While praise and commendation motivate and inspire, negative feedback is necessary for growth. That's why in chapter four, I encouraged you to view negative feedback as a gift.

But when it comes time to deliver criticism, you should realize most people won't see things this way. People tend to view negative feedback as an attack, leading them to respond in kind. Fear of this type of confrontation can hold you back from telling others what they desperately need to hear.

"We're worried about the other person's reaction," explains Erika Andersen, author of *Growing Great Employees*, in a piece she wrote for *Forbes*. "What if she gets angry? What if he cries? What if she tells me I'm an idiot? What if he gets super defensive and starts blaming *me*? Another thing that makes it hard is not knowing what to say. 'I can't actually tell that person I think he has a bad attitude,' we say to ourselves. 'He'll just tell me he has great attitude, and that I don't understand/like/respect him, and it will go from bad to worse.'"

To deal with this fear of confrontation, many resort to the sandwich method of delivering feedback. You begin by sharing something positive, followed by criticism, and conclude on a positive note. But there are problems with this strategy: Some will see through your attempts at commendation and tune them out. They know it's not the real purpose of the message, so the positive feedback goes to waste, even if it was sincere. For others, the opposite happens: they only hear the good, and the points that need improvement don't even register.

But if you ditch the sandwich method, how should you deliver negative feedback? I've found the following method effective:

1. Give the other person a chance to express themself.
By giving your communication partner a degree of control, you put them at ease. Additionally, you'll learn details regarding how they see the situation, which can help you moving forward.

2. Acknowledge their feelings and empathize.
If they admit to running into difficulty, you can share your struggle with similar circumstances and how others have helped you in the past.

3. Use appropriate questions.
The right question can help you learn more about what's going on in the other person's mind and indicate knowledge or perspective gaps. If there *is* something wrong and they can't see it, you can ask permission to share what you or others have noticed.

4. Thank the other person for listening.
Rather than commend the person for something unrelated, simply thank them for being open to hearing your feedback.

By helping the recipient to see your comments as helpful rather than harmful, you transform your feedback from destructive to constructive.

What might this look like in real life? Imagine the following scenario.

You hold a management role at work and Jenny, a member of your team, recently delivered a presentation with some major flaws. You set up a time to discuss.

YOU: "Jenny, thanks for your presentation yesterday. I wanted to get your thoughts. How do you feel it went?"

JENNY: "To be honest, I struggle so much with presenting. I always do lots of prep, and I know this stuff like the back of my hand. But I get so nervous in front of a group. My confidence drops, I start stammering... the next thing you know, I'm second-guessing everything."

YOU: "I see. Sorry to hear it was such a tough experience. You know, I still get nervous giving presentations myself."

JENNY: "Seriously? But you seem so polished up there."

YOU: "Thanks. I've had a lot of practice over the years. You mentioned taking enough time to prepare; that's great— it's probably the single best thing you can do. Can I ask: How did you prepare this time?"

JENNY: "For one thing, I did all the slides myself—because I had a very specific vision for how the message should come across. I was done weeks ago, other than minor tweaks. I must have gone over those slides a thousand times in my head."

YOU: "I see. Did you ever practice the presentation out loud, before we heard it?"

JENNY: "Um... no, I didn't."

YOU: "I never used to do that either, until someone advised me to. I've found it really helps—a presentation always sounds differently in my head than the first time I say it out loud. Also, as I hear myself speak I realize that some things may make sense to me, but not to others who aren't as familiar with the topic. If you can get someone to hear you go through a dry run, that's even better."

JENNY: "Wow. That's very helpful, thanks."

YOU: "You're welcome. Thanks to you, too—for expressing yourself openly and being willing to take in feedback. Not everyone's able to do that, you know."

JENNY: "Thank you!"

Remember, this isn't a specific formula for every situation; hopefully, it's a starting point.

Additionally, when sharing your concerns, you should give the other person the chance to respond. Be open to the possibility that you've missed something or even that you may have contributed to an undesirable situation. (In the above conversation, Jenny could have shot back: "I wanted to practice, but with all the extra work you threw on me, I had no time!") Don't focus on whether or not the other person is *wrong*; rather, concentrate on how to make things better.

Once you've established a certain level of trust in the relationship, you can be more straightforward when it comes time to offer corrective feedback. Since the recipient already sees you as someone on their side, they're more likely to understand that any comments you share are in their best interests. When speaking to these individuals, you could simply ask: "Would you be willing to hear some constructive feedback?" Then, keep it short and sweet.

Finally, don't forget: if you see someone making progress, be sure to tell them so. This will reinforce the positive behavior.

I learned lots about the power of good feedback from one of my first bosses. Marc was good-natured with a great sense of humor—usually focused on the positive and looking for things to commend.

But when we messed up, he had no problem letting us know. Sometimes it was: "Let's go for a walk." Other times it felt more like getting called to the principal's office. But I always felt that Marc cared. He wanted the department to succeed, but he wanted me to succeed, too. Years later, as I talk to some of my old colleagues, we all feel the same way.

Learning to give great feedback—both positive and negative—completely alters the effect you have on others. You're not the clueless boss who doesn't "get" your people, the spouse or parent who's impossible to please. Instead, you're the one looking out for those under your care, the one who's got their backs, the one who makes them better.

Building relationships, one step (and thank-you note) at a time

When American business executive Douglas Conant took over as the president and CEO of Campbell's Soup in 2001, he was faced with a formidable task. "The company's stock was falling steeply," writes leadership expert and bestselling author Roger Dean Duncan in a profile for *Fast Company*. "Of all the major food companies in the world, Campbell's was the rock bottom performer. Conant's challenge was to lead the company back to greatness."

To many, the assignment seemed near impossible. Conant himself described the company culture as "toxic." According to Duncan, employees were discouraged, management was dysfunctional, and trust was practically nonexistent.

Yet, somehow, Conant achieved the impossible. In less than a decade, the company had completed a remarkable turnaround and was outperforming the S&P 500. Sales and earnings rose. Employee engagement went from among the worst in the Fortune 500 to one of the best, as the company won multiple awards.

So, how did Conant do it?

Simply put, the chief executive focused on establishing trust. He communicated well, set the example, praised sincerely and specifically, and delivered on his promises.

For example, shortly after taking over, Conant began a signature practice: he put a pedometer on his belt, strapped on his walking shoes, and interacted meaningfully with as many employees as possible. "His goal was to log 10,000 steps a day," relates Duncan. "These brief encounters had multiple benefits. They helped him stay informed with the goings-on throughout the company. They enabled him to connect personally with people at every level. They enabled people to put a human face on the company's strategy and direction."

Conant also handwrote up to twenty notes a day to employees celebrating their achievements. "Most cultures don't do a good job of celebrating contributions," says Conant. "So I developed the practice of writing notes to our employees. Over 10 years, it amounted to more than 30,000 notes, and we had only 20,000 employees. Wherever I'd go in the world, in employee cubicles you'd find my handwritten notes posted on their bulletin boards."

Duncan sums up the lessons learned from Conant's success story:

"Messages matter. Repetition matters. Clarity matters. And personal touch matters... At a time when the information age has morphed into the interruption age, great leaders like Doug Conant learn to look at daily interactions through a fresh lens. Every interaction—whether it's planned or spontaneous, casual or choreographed, in a conference room or on a factory floor—is an opportunity to exercise change-friendly leadership."

And, we might add, an opportunity to build strong relationships based on trust.

Building a bridge that lasts

Trust is the foundation upon which the happiest marriages are built, the intangible quality that makes the best teams click. It's why you're willing to listen to your hairstylist or interior decorator—and it's how great companies build exceptional customer loyalty.

Deep, long-lasting trust requires connecting with others on an emotional level. But this won't happen overnight, and it won't occur by chance. Trust results when a person is able to demonstrate they are trustworthy. It is a confidence inspired by those who prove they will help, not harm—a belief in the captains who refuse to abandon ship, and the crewmates who stand beside them. Sometimes, it requires going above and beyond. Other times, it's just finding a way to hang on.

But it's always about showing up.

Every promise you deliver upon, every humble act you commit, every word of sincere and specific praise you utter, and every effort to show empathy will contribute to building deep and trusting relationships—like the untold number of delicate brushstrokes that make up a beautiful painting.

Beware, though: while trust may take years to cultivate, it can be destroyed in an instant. One lie can negate years of truth-telling; a single harsh criticism can change a relationship forever.

Of course, mistakes will be made. So, when others fall, help them up. If you keep your own failings in mind, you'll find it easier to encourage and build up rather than dishearten and tear down. By choosing to focus on the positive, skillfully sharing your own experience, or simply reminding the person that everyone has a bad day, you'll not only make the best of a bad situation—you'll win others' trust, and you'll inspire them to be the best version of themselves.

Usually, they'll be more than willing to return the favor.

8

The Dark Side

From Dr. Jekyll to Mr. Hyde

* * * * *

The power to do good is also the power to do harm.

MILTON FRIEDMAN

T HE MID-TWENTIETH CENTURY saw one of the most peculiar and horrific developments in human history. Adolf Hitler, a socially awkward artist-turned-soldier, steadily climbed Germany's political ladder, building influence along the way. As a newfound dictator, he led his country into World War II and subsequently orchestrated one of the largest genocides in history.

But how did Hitler rise to power in a democratic country?

After losing World War I, Germany was thrown into chaos and devastation. The economy was in shambles, and unemployment was high. German patriots and veterans felt their politicians had betrayed them. Hitler offered a scapegoat: hundreds of thousands of Jews who had integrated into German society but who were largely perceived as outsiders. He blamed these immigrants and other marginalized populations for Germany's problems and began laying out a plan to restore the country to greatness.

Especially notable was Hitler's ability to tap into the negative emotions of fear, anger, and resentment and use these to gain support from the masses. A gifted orator who spoke with confidence and charisma, Hitler would rehearse his speeches meticulously, practicing not only his words but also his facial expressions and hand gestures. He coaxed his followers into a fervor. As Hitler's speeches began attracting increasingly larger crowds, his reputation and influence grew.

Eventually, Hitler managed to gain full control of the legislative and executive branches of government, using this power to dissolve freedom of the press, eliminate rival parties, and pass discriminatory laws. In 1934, Hitler became the sole leader of Germany.

"Disturbingly, many of Hitler's early measures didn't require mass repression," explain Alex Gendler and Anthony Hazard in the short film, *How Did Hitler Rise to Power?* "His speeches exploited people's fear and ire to drive their support behind him and the Nazi party. Meanwhile, businessmen and intellectuals, wanting to be on the right side of public opinion, endorsed Hitler. They assured themselves and each other that his more extreme rhetoric was only for show."

Hitler's ability to evoke, intensify, and even manipulate the emotions of his followers highlights a harsh and important reality: emotional intelligence also has a dark side.

Breaking bad

Until now, I've focused on the more positive uses of a high EQ, such as how it can help you manage conflict or establish deeper relationships. But it's important to remember that emotional intelligence, much like "traditional" intelligence, is not inherently virtuous. It's a tool.

In other words, emotional intelligence can be used for good *or* evil.

As you know, emotional intelligence is the ability to use knowledge of emotions to inform and guide behavior, usually to reach a goal. But these goals can differ drastically from person to person. For example, we've discussed the benefits of sincere and specific praise, but what if a person commends others just to gain more power for themselves or to gather support for a suspect cause? What if they use their ability to express (or disguise) emotions in an attempt to manipulate others? A person in a position of power or authority could also use fear and pressure as intimidation tactics.

For example, consider the following scenarios:

· A public figure or pundit who makes intentionally outrageous and inflammatory remarks in an attempt to garner media attention or gain a following

· A husband or wife who hides an extramarital affair in order to string along their mate and possibly lover

· A manager or employee who distorts the truth or purposefully spreads rumors to gain a psychological advantage over others

In one research paper, a team of management professors compared this type of behavior to that of Iago, the antagonist in Shakespeare's *Othello*. They describe Iago as "a man who manipulates others' emotions while controlling his own" in his efforts to completely destroy his adversaries.

This is what we call the dark side of emotional intelligence: using one's knowledge of emotions to strategically achieve self-serving goals, with little or no concern for others. Much as a person possessing a brilliant intellect could become an accomplished detective or a criminal mastermind, one with a superior EQ has a choice between two very different paths.

In this chapter, we're going to explore the dark side. You'll see more real-life examples of individuals who have used their ability to influence others' emotions for selfish gain. You'll learn why the line between ethical and unethical influence isn't always so clear—and how even a person with good motive could turn to outright manipulation, dishonesty, or hypocrisy. Finally, I'll describe some of the specific manipulative techniques others use in trying to turn your emotions against you, and how to protect yourself when they do.

Psychopaths and narcissists and manipulators, oh my

The term "psychopath" may evoke images of serial killers or mass murderers. But the complex disorder known as psychopathy—which is traditionally characterized by a list of traits including antisocial behavior, arrogance, deceitfulness, and a lack of emotional empathy—is actually more common than most people think.

A criminal psychologist, Professor Robert Hare spent most of his life studying psychopaths and learning what makes them tick.* In an interview with the *Telegraph*, Hare described psychopathy as "dimensional," suggesting that many psychopaths tend to blend in. "There are people who are part-way up the scale, high enough to warrant an assessment for psychopathy,

---

* Hare is the creator of the Psychopathy Checklist—Revised (PCL-R), the assessment most commonly used to identify psychopathic traits in an individual.

but not high enough up to cause problems. Often they're our friends, they're fun to be around. They might take advantage of us now and then, but usually it's subtle and they're able to talk their way around it."

Hare claims that psychopathic traits can even appear advantageous in some circumstances. For example, some individuals excel in the workplace because of their charisma and ability to manipulate others. In some cases, a manager may even mistakenly attribute leadership traits to what are actually psychopathic behaviors.

"Taking charge, making decisions, and getting others to do what you want are classic features of leadership and management, yet they can also be well-packaged forms of coercion, domination, and manipulation," explain Hare and his co-author Paul Babiak in the book *Snakes in Suits: When Psychopaths Go to Work*. "One might think that abusive, deceitful behavior toward coworkers would eventually lead to disciplinary action and termination. But, based on the cases we have reviewed, this is often not the case."

Of course, it's not only psychopaths who misuse the abilities of emotional influence for selfish gain.

Consider the following examples:

- A group of German scientists found that individuals who demonstrated certain narcissistic traits (characterized as demonstrating a pervasive pattern of grandiosity, self-focus, and self-importance) made better first impressions on their peers by using humor and charming facial expressions.

- A 2011 study indicated that "Machiavellians" (people who show a tendency to manipulate others for personal gain) who rated high in knowledge of emotion-regulation were more likely to engage in deviant actions, such as publicly embarrassing someone at work.

• A 2013 study found that those who tended to exploit others for personal gain were also good at reading those peoples' emotions, especially negative ones.

To illustrate how this type of behavior can infect culture on a large scale, consider the troubles of what was until recently one of the most respected companies in America.

Profiting from emotional sabotage

In September 2016, news broke that employees working for Wells Fargo, one of the largest and most successful banks in the world, had blatantly deceived millions of customers through a variety of illegal business practices, including secretly applying for over 565,000 credit cards that customers never asked for; opening about 3.5 million unauthorized bank accounts, resulting in millions of dollars in customer fees; creating fraudulent email accounts to sign up customers for additional services; and transferring customers' money back and forth between accounts, without permission.

In response to these actions, Wells Fargo was initially fined $185 million by the Consumer Financial Protection Bureau. It also agreed to pay around $110 million in a resulting class-action lawsuit (in addition to millions in legal fees) and suffered extensive, long-term damage to its reputation.

In today's cutthroat business climate, it's easy to imagine a few rogue employees engaging in unscrupulous behavior. But you might wonder: How did over five thousand people become involved in such brazen, widespread deception?

An independent investigation into the company's sales practices revealed a telling conclusion:

"The root cause of sales practice failures was the distortion of the Community Bank's sales culture and performance management system, which, *when combined with aggressive sales management, created pressure on employees* to sell unwanted or unneeded products to customers and, in some cases, to open unauthorized accounts." (Italics mine.)

"I had managers in my face yelling at me," said Sabrina Bertrand, who worked as a licensed personal banker for Wells Fargo in Houston in 2013. "They wanted you to open up dual checking accounts for people that couldn't even manage their original checking account. The sales pressure from management was unbearable."

Erik, who worked at the Wells Fargo corporate headquarters branch in San Francisco, said that employees were pressured constantly to sell bank products (accounts, credit cards, loans). Workers who struggled to meet their daily quotas were "reprimanded and told to do whatever it takes."

"It was multiple occasions where I saw my co-workers were cracking under the pressure," he said. "Tears, crying, constantly getting pulled into the back room having one-on-ones for coaching sessions."

One employee we'll call Monica, who also worked at the headquarters branch, described these agonizing coaching sessions. Two managers would escort Monica to a room with no windows, then lock the door. They instructed her to sit down at a large conference table, handed her a "formal warning," and requested she sign it.

"If you don't meet your solutions, you're not a team player," said the managers. "If you're bringing down the team then you will be fired and it will be on your permanent record." Monica, who was in her early twenties, says she feared starting her career off on the wrong foot, especially in the middle of a financial crisis. "You were stuck and it was the feeling that no other employer is going to want you because we will ruin you," she related.

What happened at Wells Fargo doesn't look like emotional intelligence the way we usually consider it. But reality is that leadership at the company used emotional manipulation and deceit—dark elements of EQ—to reach their goals. While it's difficult to estimate just how much restitution Wells Fargo will be required to make, at least two top executives who were judged culpable in the scandal walked away from the company with millions of dollars in compensation.*

What stands out about these stories isn't the unscrupulous behavior; it's the fact that Wells got caught in its web of deceit, and that the company as a whole was publicly shamed for its actions. Unfortunately, countless others get away with such emotional profiteering every day.

But is all emotional manipulation so easy to spot?

Protect yourself

Attempts to influence your emotions appear in many forms. For example, consider the following examples:

Watch a few commercials or step inside any store, and you'll experience the efforts of retailers to persuade. Marketing departments spend millions to bombard you daily with clever language and beautiful images, all designed to reach you on an emotional level, to stimulate a craving for the latest and greatest, to make you feel that you must have their product *right this second*. Companies collect vast amounts of data, essentially tracking your every move, so they can personalize the ad experience and encourage you to buy more.

Business leaders often try to leverage the power of emotion to reach their goals. In one study on emotional behavior, Stanford professor Joanne Martin and her team spent time

---

* According to *Fortune*, after factoring in benefits and total compensation, former Wells CEO John Stumpf was required to return 40 percent of the $174 million he collected from Wells Fargo upon retiring. Former consumer banking chief Carrie Tolstedt was required to return 54 percent of her $125 million pay package.

with employees of multinational retailer the Body Shop. At one point, founder and former CEO Anita Roddick identified an employee's tendency to break down and cry when frustrated. The chief executive saw this as a strategic opportunity and told the employee this "has to be used." Roddick then encouraged the employee to channel that emotion, directing her specifically when she should cry in an upcoming meeting.

In 2012, Facebook conducted a one-week experiment to see how users would respond to changes in their newsfeeds. Some were shown content that was deemed more happy and positive; others were shown content identified as more negative. But as details of the experiment emerged, the general public was outraged, seeing Facebook's experimentation as flagrant emotional manipulation.

Of course, every day you'll face attempts by people who are intent on influencing your behavior, most efforts more mundane than these. Sometimes such attempts will be obvious: a romantic partner who sulks when they don't get their way, a colleague who throws a temper tantrum to influence the boss. Other times they'll be more subtle—perhaps even using some of the very tools and methods we've discussed in earlier chapters.

So, we might ask: How can you deal effectively with others' attempts to influence you?

Here is where your social awareness skills come into play. For example, your capacity to accurately perceive others' abilities to manage emotions can serve as a self-defense mechanism—a type of "emotional alarm system" that alerts you to the fact that someone is attempting to manipulate your feelings, to get you to act in a way that is not in your best interests or that conflicts with your values and principles.

Let's explore some of the unscrupulous methods individuals use to exploit your emotions and see how your own emotional intelligence can combat them.

Fear

Some manipulators work hard to create or exploit fear in an effort to scare you into action. They may do so subtly, through deceit or exaggeration, or directly, by means of threats or even verbal abuse.

> **TRY THIS:** Strive to identify situations where others use fear to influence your feelings and actions. We tend to fear the unknown; therefore, research the facts and consider opposing opinions before passing judgment or making a decision. Endeavor to see the whole picture. If you're the victim of abuse, don't face it alone; seek help from someone you trust.

It's not possible to completely eliminate all of our fears, but identifying and preparing to face them inspires confidence.

Anger

In chapter two, I outlined some techniques for dealing with negative emotions. But what if someone is intentionally trying to get you riled up? Maybe it's a competitor who tries to throw you off your game or an online troll seeking attention or entertainment.

Dr. Drew Brannon has spent over a decade advising high-level athletes, teams, and coaches on how to deal with trash talk: the things competitors say in an attempt to challenge your beliefs or erode your confidence. "If someone is trying to get in your head," Brannon told me, "it should build your confidence in some respect, because it confirms that you are a threat to them and their objectives."

The problem comes when that person succeeds in manipulating you, which could lead to irrational or regrettable decisions.

➤ **TRY THIS:** How you choose to engage with these people depends much on the situation and what you hope to accomplish. If dealing with a competitor, for example, it helps to think ahead and prepare for how you will react to attempts to get you angry. Brannon calls this skill "Green Light."

"With Green Light, I teach clients to have a plan, a preestablished routine of how to respond to trash talk," said Brannon. "With this type of programmed response, you know exactly where to go with your thoughts when opponents talk trash, helping you stay focused on the task at hand. Green Light works because our minds function best when we know we have the ability to meet a challenge. When the moment comes, you simply do what you've trained for."

You can adopt a similar approach with online trolls, especially if they're anonymous. While I generally discourage engaging with trolls or overly aggressive online personalities, you may be inclined to do so in specific circumstances. (Keep in mind that many trolls aren't even real people—they may be computer-generated chat bots or individuals hired to play a role, with the goal to sow seeds of discord and influence public opinion.) In these cases, skillful use of the tools of influence outlined in chapter six (showing personal interest, communicating with respect, reasoning with empathy) can help you deal with such people as effectively as possible. But if the other party continues their aggression, it's time to ignore and move on.

Excitement

Recent events have shone a spotlight on the potential for false stories to spread at an unprecedented rate. Rumors and misinformation were always a problem, but modern technology has increased the potential for such falsehoods to reach more people at a quicker rate.

When individuals read a story or watch a video that reinforces their own strong emotions, they will often share that video through social media or other channels. The more people share, the more believable the story becomes. Additionally, consider the rapidly evolving media landscape, where numerous publishers are funded by pay-per-click advertising. More readers of an article equals more customers (and more revenue), giving rise to sensational and biased reporting.

The result is an environment where more and more people are striving to manipulate your emotions. Individuals or special-interest groups often contribute to a false or biased narrative, either to spread their personal ideology or to benefit financially.

> **TRY THIS:** Rather than immediately believing or sharing a story, image, or video, consider the following:

1. What's the source?
If a source is anonymous, it can be difficult to determine the truth of what is presented. Information that's presented on record and that's traceable is typically more reliable.

"Also be wary of organizations that blindly quote other organizations without solid sourcing," says Ian Fisher, assistant managing editor for digital operations at the *New York*

Times. "They aren't taking a very big chance in doing that. They can always say 'Oh, that was them, not us.'"

2. What's the context?

Even if you read a direct quote or see (or hear) a person speaking or taking action, it can be difficult to understand a situation without knowing the context. What is the overall point the person is trying to make? What extenuating circumstances may have contributed to what you saw or heard? These questions may help you better understand a situation before commenting on it.

3. How sensational is it?

If a story seems unbelievable, there's a high probability that it is.*

Further, it's important to gauge the degree of bias from any third-party reporting. Does the narrative only provide one side of the story? Is it extreme in its attempt to praise or discredit others? Who would benefit from the story if it spread? Might the source have ulterior motives?

4. How are other sources reporting the story?

"If a news organization says 'we can confirm that such and such has happened,' pay attention to what the other networks are saying," says Andy Carvin, senior strategist on

---

* In 2017, the *Guardian* reported on "a new breed of video and audio manipulation tools, made possible by advances in artificial intelligence and computer graphics," which allows for the creation of realistic-looking footage that is based on deceit. For example, software developed at Stanford University was used to manipulate video footage of public figures. The software would capture a second person's facial expressions as they spoke into a webcam and then morph those movements directly onto the face of the public figure in the original video. Then, using another piece of software, a team was able to take three to five minutes of audio of a victim's voice (say, ripped from a YouTube video) and create a voice match close enough that it could even fool voice biometric security systems used by some banks and smartphones. The result was realistic video footage of those public figures appearing to say things that, in reality, they never said.

NPR's Digital Desk. "Because ideally you can triangulate that information and get to some nugget of truth. But the fewer examples you have of entities claiming that something has happened, the more wary you should be about it."

5. Do I really need to share this?

Remember the tools you've already learned, including the pause and the use of questions: Does this need to be said? Does this need to be said by me? Does this need to be said by me now?

Taking just a few moments may prevent you from spreading false information and help you avoid the need to later retract or delete.

Confusion

At times, a person may try to confuse you in an attempt to gain an advantage. There are various ways to do this; for example, they might speak at a faster pace, use vocabulary you're not familiar with, or consistently deny something you know to be true.

➤ **TRY THIS:** If you're unclear about something, ask the other person to slow down or repeat what they've said. Then, continue to ask questions until you understand. You can also repeat their point in your words or ask them to name an example—allowing you to regain control of the conversation. Finally, don't be afraid to seek a second and third opinion from people you trust.

Reciprocity

Simply put, reciprocity describes our desire to give something back to someone who has done something for us. If someone buys us a gift or performs a favor, we feel obligated to respond in-kind.

The problem is that some people use the "rule of reciprocity" to exploit others, as psychology professor Robert Cialdini explains in his classic bestselling book *Influence*. "Because there is general distaste for those who take and make no effort to give in return, we will often go to great lengths to avoid being considered one of their number," he says. "It is to those lengths that we will often be taken and, in the process, be 'taken' by individuals who stand to gain from our indebtedness."

For example, a person may seek to do small favors for you while asking for much bigger ones in return. Or, they may shower you with lavish gifts or excessive praise for the sole reason of trying to curry favor or influence.

➤ **TRY THIS:** Be careful from whom you accept gifts or favors, and be wary of those who only seem to give when they want something back in return. The goal shouldn't be to refuse or be skeptical of *all* generosity, which would rob you of genuine opportunities to experience the kindness or helpfulness of others. Instead, take into account the relationship you have with the giver, as well as their possible motives.

Additionally, training yourself to identify how others exploit the rule of reciprocity will give you the emotional fortitude you need to avoid getting played.

Social proof and peer pressure

When individuals are uncertain, they will look to the actions of others to help them make decisions. This type of social proof can be positive, as it helps prevent unruly behavior.

At times, though, a person or group may use social proof to pressure you to act against your values or principles. For example, think of the professional athlete who convinces a teammate to take performance-enhancing drugs because "everyone is doing it."

> **TRY THIS:** If you consistently take time to revisit and reflect on your values, you can develop the conviction you need to stay by them, even in the face of pressure from others. Additionally, using the techniques discussed in chapter two (like the pause and the fast-forward) will help you think through your decisions—instead of following a crowd that's headed in the wrong direction.

Passive-aggressive behavior

Passive-aggressive behavior is the display of negative feelings, resentment, and aggression in an unassertive or "passive" manner. It may be characterized by consistent procrastination or avoidance of emotional conversation, or by subtle comments or actions that indicate displeasure.

It includes actions such as the following:

· Refusing to acknowledge genuine feelings of anger
· Sulking
· Giving the silent treatment

- Verbally complying with a request to appease others, but not following through (or using procrastination for the express purpose of getting out of a task)
- Intentionally carrying out a task in a way that is below expectations
- Claiming ignorance
- Giving backhanded compliments
- Responding with sarcasm

Many people who regularly employ passive-aggressive behavior may not even realize they're doing so. But that doesn't make their behavior easier to bear.

➤ **TRY THIS:** Signe Whitson, co-author of *The Angry Smile*, advises that the only way to truly address passive-aggressiveness is to confront it:

"It's not an in-your-face, anger-inspiring, make-them-admit-what-they-did kind of authoritarian tactic but rather a quiet and reflective verbal intervention skill in which a person gently but openly shares his or her thoughts about the other person's behavior and unexpressed anger."

To do this, be sure to clearly communicate your own feelings and expectations. If you suspect that you know the specific cause of the other person's aggression, ask specifically if that's what's bothering them. If they deny that's the case, take their word for it. But gently try to keep the discussion going. Take initiative to apologize for anything you've done that could contribute to hurt feelings and ask what you could do to make the situation better.

Once the problem is identified, work together to find an agreement that satisfies both parties moving forward.

The love bomb

"Love bombing is an attempt to influence another person with over-the-top displays of attention and affection," writes psychiatrist Dale Archer. Unlike healthy relationships, he explains, in which displays of affection continue indefinitely and actions match words, love bombing often involves "an abrupt shift in the type of attention, from affectionate and loving to controlling and angry, with the pursuing partner making unreasonable demands."

Archer and other medical professionals have identified the love bomb as a weapon, a form of psychological manipulation that is used to maintain power and control in a relationship. Pimps and gang leaders use it to encourage loyalty and obedience. Cult leaders have practiced it to coerce followers into mass suicide. And more than a few individuals use love bombing to abuse romantic partners.

How do you combat sinister uses of emotional intelligence? By working to increase your own.

➤ **TRY THIS:** Keeping in mind that it takes time to build trust in a relationship, beware of those who constantly seek to stroke your ego, push a relationship to levels you're not ready for, or are quick to show warmth and affection but then quickly lose their temper or find other ways to "punish" you when they don't get their way.

If a relationship seems to be moving too fast, don't be afraid to slow things down. And don't be afraid to say no when appropriate. If you feel that you're already deeply involved in an unhealthy or abusive relationship, talk about it with trusted family or friends, or seek professional help.

Of course, these are just a few techniques of emotional manipulation, but this list is far from exhaustive. How can you defend yourself from similar tactics?

Remember that knowledge is power. Aim to build self- and social awareness by learning the different ways others can use emotions against you. Then strive to balance your instinctive, emotional reactions with solid reasoning and rational thinking—using the various techniques you've learned in this book.

How courage and resilience created a tipping point

We recently witnessed a real-life demonstration of the battle between the two sides of emotional intelligence, dark and light, as a large number of brave women (and some men) came forward to speak about sexual harassment and assault in the workplace.

The inspiration for this large-scale reckoning has been largely attributed to a *New York Times* article that reported substantial allegations of sexual misconduct against famed Hollywood producer Harvey Weinstein. Multiple women claimed that Weinstein used his power and influence in the film industry to try to coerce them into sexual favors.

Over the following weeks, allegations of misogynistic behavior increased exponentially—ranging from intimidation techniques to outright harassment and even assault. Dozens of powerful men across industries resigned or were fired as multiple accusations piled up against them, leading to what eventually became known as "the Weinstein effect."

What resulted was a true watershed moment. Millions used the social media hashtag #MeToo, a phrase developed by women's advocate Tarana Burke and popularized by actress Alyssa Milano, to add their voices to the conversation. Untold numbers of victims were inspired to come forward and share their personal stories of abuse, forcing a silent pandemic into the limelight. Friends, family members, and colleagues everywhere began speaking about the problem, its causes, and how to prevent it.

But why now? Why was this horrific problem suddenly getting the attention it has desperately needed all of these years?

It's difficult to say, but it seems that history has been leading up to this moment.

For years, so many women were afraid to speak out about their experience. This was due to various reasons: fear of not being taken seriously (or not being believed), fear of being shamed or ridiculed, fear of retaliation. Fear that a single moment—one that was forced upon them—could end up defining the rest of their lives.

But more and more women have spoken up about their battles against sexual misconduct over the past decades. In turn, these women inspired others to share their stories. As those conversations gained momentum, many victims realized that rather than being alone, they were the overwhelming majority.

And as those voices joined together, they became progressively louder—until they formed a crack that eventually burst the dam.

Writer Sophie Gilbert put it eloquently in a piece she wrote for the *Atlantic*:

"There's a monumental amount of work to be done in confronting a climate of serial sexual predation—one in which women are belittled and undermined and abused and sometimes pushed out of their industries altogether. But uncovering the colossal scale of the problem is revolutionary in its own right."

Fight the power

At some point, you will cross paths with those who attempt to use dark traits of emotional intelligence for personal gain. Some of them are purposefully scheming and manipulative. Others simply believe they are trying to reach a goal. In either case, you must remember: *you* are in control of your emotional reactions.

Emotions like anger and fear can cause major damage—especially if you rush to judgment before learning the facts. Once you are emotionally attached to your beliefs, it becomes more difficult to remain objective. That's why you must continue to use your ability to think—together with your emotions—to make sure your beliefs are based on truth.

To be clear, my goal isn't to encourage undue suspicion or to paint a picture of you versus the world. But I advise you to be cautious—and even skeptical—when necessary. Rather than consider every encounter a zero-sum game, view them as learning opportunities—chances to improve your own emotional intelligence. When you discover that someone has the ability to evoke strong emotions in you, acknowledge that power; yet, strive to remain balanced with respect to your own words and actions. Once your own feelings have calmed down, revisit the "what" and the "why": What words or actions sparked your emotions? Why did they do so? What are the influencer's true motives and desires?

To be persuaded, motivated, and influenced by others can be a good thing—as long as it results in behavior that is consistent with your values. If it doesn't—if you discover you've been duped or victimized—endeavor to understand where you went wrong and how you can avoid repeating the mistake. With practice, you'll continually build both self- and social awareness, and you'll gain greater control over your thoughts and actions. Doing so will help keep you from becoming a slave to your feelings, even if a skilled manipulator works hard to exploit you.

Above all, remember: the best way to protect yourself from harmful uses of emotional intelligence is by striving to increase your own.

That statement, though, comes with a caveat: as your ability to manage and influence emotions increases, it becomes a source of power—and power corrupts. As we have seen, some of the world's most notorious figures have demonstrated evidence of high emotional intelligence, at least certain traits of it. Was it self-interest that motivated them to sharpen these skills? Or did their emotional abilities fuel their self-interest? At what point does the attempt to manage others' emotions become unethical?

Pondering those questions reminds us that emotional intelligence is only one piece of the puzzle.

Work hard to sharpen your EQ and put it into practice—but don't do so at the expense of your principles. Rather, use your moral compass to direct your efforts and allow ethics and values to guide your development.

Do all this, and hopefully you will avoid falling victim to the dark side.

9

Moving Forward

Embracing the Emotional Journey

• • • • •

You are beautiful because you let yourself feel,
and that is a brave thing indeed.

SHINJI MOON

THROUGHOUT THIS BOOK, I've endeavored to establish why emotional intelligence is so important and teach specific methods to help you increase your own EQ. You've seen that while it's vital to understand emotions and how they work, even more critical is being able to use that knowledge to effectively reach your goals.

You've discovered how taking time to ask the right questions—to both yourself and others—can help build self- and social awareness, and how learning to control your thoughts can help you manage your emotions more effectively. You've learned not only what an emotional hijack is but how to escape it, and why you should view almost all feedback as a gift—because it provides an opportunity to learn and improve.

Hopefully, you've picked up practical knowledge that can inform your EQ-development strategies for the future. For example, that by designing healthy habits to replace destructive ones, you can proactively shape your emotional reactions over time—in effect, rewiring your brain. Also, that by demonstrating qualities like authenticity, humility, and respect, you can inspire others to show the same qualities in return. Don't forget the value of emotionally intelligent empathy—the kind that builds rapport and aids your ability to connect with others but that doesn't lead to emotional exhaustion.

Moving forward, I encourage you to look for the various ways emotional intelligence manifests itself in your day-to-day life.

Maybe it's through your favorite barista, whose smile and conversation skills always put you in a good mood. Or, maybe it's in the friend, family member, or colleague who is always ready to lend an empathetic ear.

You might see it in the actions of a small child, like I did the other day. Noticing I wasn't myself, my little boy sat down next to me, gently placed his arm around my shoulder, and looked me straight in the eye before saying, "I love you, Dad." Four simple words, but powerful enough to change my mood in an instant.

But as you've learned, seeing others' EQ in action won't always leave you with a warm, pleasant feeling. It may rear its head in an ugly way—in the form of a co-worker who pushes your buttons to get their way, or an internet troll who tries to get you riled up. When this happens, remember to apply what you've learned.

As you continue the emotional journey, you'll realize that in many ways our feelings are a contradiction. All of us have experienced both love and hate, joy and sadness, courage and fear. This common ground should bond us as humans;

however, those same emotions often create conflict, separating us in the end. But if there's one thing I've learned through the years, it's this: we are all far more alike than we are different. The differences simply give us a chance to learn.

Consider my friend Jill, who is known for her tendency to say the first thing that comes to her mind—which sometimes leads to a bad first impression or an apparent faux pas. Often, Jill doesn't recognize the impact her words have on others, and that lack of social awareness certainly hurts her at times.

But Jill's impulsive communication style is also a strength. If there is something difficult to be said, Jill has no problem saying it—like telling a person to go find a breath mint if they need it. She also isn't afraid to wear her heart on her sleeve, which produces a curious result: others are drawn to her. Many appreciate Jill's authenticity because it's usually expressed with good intention. They feel comfortable with her, knowing they can let their guard down as she does with them.

Over time, I realized that these traits give Jill an incredible ability to reach people in a way few others do, a power to motivate and influence. Almost everyone who gets to know her adores her and is happy to follow her lead.

As someone who naturally struggles with confrontation, I've learned a lot from Jill. She's taught me the value of speaking up for the greater good, even if doing so initially makes others uncomfortable. And while I continue to extol the benefits of thoughtful communication, Jill has taught me not to overthink my words and actions.

This is the lesson you must strive to keep in mind: emotional intelligence comes in all different packages, shapes, and sizes. Man or woman. Quiet or loud. Brash or meek. Leader or follower.

As you become aware of your own emotional tendencies and weaknesses, endeavor to learn from those who are the most different from you.

Because in many cases, it's those people who can teach you the most.

A final word

Our emotions influence practically everything about our lives. They determine whether or not we enjoy a movie, a song, or a piece of art. They help us decide which career path we take, for which jobs we apply. They impact our decisions as to where we will live and for how long. They help us determine with whom we choose to spend our time, whom we date, whom we fall in love with and marry... and whom we leave behind.

Emotions can cause us to make a split-second decision, with consequences that will follow us for the rest of our lives. At times, they make us feel like we're stuck in a black hole with no way out—even if in the eyes of the rest of the world we've got it made. But they can also provide light at the end of the tunnel, making the most dire of circumstances more bearable.

Emotions determine how we choose our leaders and how our leaders choose us. They've motivated every war that's ever been fought—and every peace treaty that's ever been signed.

It is for all these reasons that emotional intelligence is so invaluable.

Remember that emotional intelligence isn't about understanding every feeling you have as it occurs or dissecting every event as it happens. Rather, it's the ability to search for deeper understanding when beneficial. And the ability to simply enjoy the moment when not.

There's no lifetime certification for EQ. Just as a musician who doesn't practice will soon become rusty, neglecting self-reflection and perspective-taking will cause you to lose your abilities over time. It's often when you feel that you've "mastered" a facet of emotional intelligence that you'll make your greatest mistakes. But it's how you handle those mistakes that will determine how emotionally intelligent you truly are. At these times, moments of reflection and practice will yield surprising insights and "aha" moments that can change you for the better, if you let them.

As these occur, please share them with me, using the contact information found at the end of this book. After all, we're all students. And we continue to learn from each other.

So, keep learning those lessons. Continue striving to harness the great power of emotion, lest you become slave to your own feelings. Pursue knowledge and understanding with the goal of making yourself better. Use that knowledge to protect yourself from those who try to take advantage of you and your feelings.

Above all, remember that emotions are beautiful. They make us human.

Enjoy them. Love them. Embrace them.

But never underestimate their power, and their potential to do harm.

Learn to live in harmony with these fundamental truths—and you'll be sure to make emotions work for you, instead of against you.

Appendix
The Ten Commandments of Emotional Intelligence

I. Thou shalt ponder thy feelings.
Emotional intelligence begins by learning to ask the right questions, like the following:

- What are my emotional strengths? What are my emotional weaknesses?
- How would I describe my communication style? How would others describe it?
- How does my current mood affect my thoughts and decision-making?
- In what situations do I find that emotions work against me?

Pondering questions like those will help you build self-awareness, which will yield valuable insights that can be used to your advantage.

II. Thou shalt learn from other perspectives.
When listening to others, don't focus on right or wrong; rather, work to understand how perceptions differ and the reasons they do.

That includes learning to take negative feedback, which can expose blind spots and lead to self-improvement.

III. Thou shalt learn to pause.

The pause is as simple as taking a moment to stop and think before you act or speak. But beware: while easy in theory, it's difficult in practice.

Don't expect perfection. Practice consistently, and the pause will prevent embarrassment and could save countless relationships.

IV. Thou shalt practice empathy.

Instead of judging or labeling others, work hard to see things through their eyes. Listen with the goal of understanding the other person and their point of view, even if you don't agree. Ask yourself: *Why does this person feel this way? What's going on beneath the surface?*

Empathy helps increase your ability to influence others and allows you to build deeper, more connected relationships.

V. Thou shalt praise others.

Humans crave sincere praise and acknowledgment. When you express appreciation for others, you satisfy that craving—and build trust in the process.

Remember, everyone deserves commendation for something. By focusing on the good in others, and then specifically telling them what you appreciate, you inspire them to be the best version of themselves.

VI. Thou shalt apologize.

"I'm sorry" can be the two most difficult words to say. But they can also be the most powerful.

Acknowledge your mistakes and apologize when appropriate, and you'll develop qualities like humility and authenticity, naturally drawing others to you.

VII. Thou shalt forgive.

Refusing to forgive is like reopening a wound—you never give yourself the chance to heal.

Instead of hanging on to resentment while the offending party moves on with their life, forgiving gives you the chance to move on, too.

VIII. Thou shalt be authentic.

Authentic people share their true thoughts and feelings with others. They know not everyone will agree with them and that this is okay. They also realize that they aren't perfect, but they're willing to show those imperfections because they know everyone else has them, too.

Authenticity doesn't mean sharing everything about your-self, with everyone, all of the time. It *does* mean saying what you mean, meaning what you say, and sticking to your values and principles above all else.

IX. Thou shalt control thy thoughts.

When you experience a negative situation, you may not have much control over your feelings. But by focusing on your thoughts, you can control your reaction to those feelings.

When you focus on your thinking, you resist becoming a slave to your emotions. Instead, acknowledge those feelings and then move forward in a way that's in harmony with your goals and values.

X. Thou shalt not stop learning.

Emotional intelligence isn't about achieving perfection or reaching a certain level of EQ. It's often when you feel you've "mastered" the other nine commandments that you will make your greatest mistakes. It is how you handle those mistakes that will determine just how emotionally intelligent you truly are.

Never underestimate the power of emotions for good, nor their potential to harm. And always strive to make emotions work for you, instead of against you.

Acknowledgments

LOOKING BACK, I'VE always found the topic of emotion fascinating. It began with my parents, who are polar opposites. I took mostly after my mom, who was quick to express her emotions. She loved to laugh and looked for opportunities to do so. She was moved almost as easily to tears. She passed this ability to feel quickly and deeply onto me, and it shaped who I am today. Among countless lessons, my mom taught me the value of empathy, for which I will be forever grateful.

My dad was different; he thrived on the feeling of control. This was evident in the way he evoked emotions in others: a great storyteller, he kept you hanging on every word—always (slowly) building to a great reveal. But that desire for control led him to hide certain emotions, lest he appear weak. (To this day, I've never seen him shed a tear.) Through my dad, I've learned that although as humans we experience the same emotions, the way we express them differs vastly from person to person.

My sister is a strong, beautiful woman who learned resilience by facing up to severe challenges, tackling them head-on, and refusing to give up. She taught me to do the same. I find her confidence inspiring.

My brother is brilliant yet humble, with an ability to express emotions in ways that I don't possess. We share a unique bond and although he's over a decade younger than me, I continue to learn from him. In many ways, I wish I were more like him.

My father-in-law is one of the warmest, most hospitable, most loving, and hardest-working people I've ever met, much like his wife was. I am eternally grateful that they accepted me into their beautiful family, and I can't wait to see Mom again.

My brother- and sister-in-law, Adam and Ella, are more than family; they're friends. In a new country, with a new language, new food, and new culture, they helped me feel at home.

A number of teachers nurtured my love of writing, but none more than Ms. Jane Glasser, who taught my senior-year literary analysis class. Ms. Glasser encouraged me to write, not just for myself, but for others.

In 1998, I was invited to New York to work at Bethel, the world headquarters of Jehovah's Witnesses. I'd go on to spend the next thirteen years of my life there, where I learned from outstanding mentors like Marc and Jess Portillo, Kevin Wier, Mark Flores, Max Larson, John Larson, John Foster, Andres Reinoso, Alex Gonzales, Duane Svenson, Jon and Janet Sharpe, Alan and Joan Janzen, Ty and Rebecca Fulton, Diane Khanna, Tony Perez, Tony Griffin, Mark Mattson, Chuck Woody, Doug Chappel, Virgil Card, Thomas Jefferson, and others. These individuals taught me that leadership isn't about position, it's about action. They also showed me that the best managers always put people first. This was a remarkable education and set of experiences that I wouldn't trade for anything.

Fausto and Vera Hidalgo, Roel and Sheryl Tuzon, Priest Price, Sandra and Orvil Hinojos, Jesse and Liz Hoefle (and their families), the Venturina family, the Figueras family, the Flores family, the Lemsic family, the Carlos family, the Myszczenko family, the Asare family, and the Romano family all gave me a home away from home, along with more than I could ever return. Each of them holds a special place in my heart.

Ms. Lisle, Belen del Valle, the Mann family, Anita Beyer, and Kris Sistrunk all helped me get a good start in Germany and taught me about doing business in Europe.

The LinkedIn writing and editing team—including Daniel Roth, Isabelle Roughol, Chip Cutter, John C. Abell, Amy Chen, Laura Lorenzetti Soper, and Katie Carroll—gave me a platform to share my thoughts and ideas, which opened up opportunities I would have never thought possible.

Jeff Haden took me under his wing and taught me more than I could have imagined about achieving success as an author—for no good reason except that he's a really nice guy.

Laura Lorber took a chance on an unproven author when she gave me a column on Inc.com. Then, she helped me grow immensely as a writer.

Daniel Goleman, Carol Dweck, Howard Gardner, Brené Brown, Satya Nadella, Howard Schultz, Captain Chesley B. "Sully" Sullenberger III, Robert Cialdini, Sheryl Sandberg, Simon Sinek, Tiffany Watt Smith, Tom Peters, Richard Davidson, Travis Bradberry, Jean Graves, Sharon Begley, Daniel Ariely, Daniel Kahneman, Victor Cheng, Joseph LeDoux, and Susan David all shared enlightening insights about emotions, the mind, or management theory and practice that have proven foundational to my own work.

Hendrie Weisinger (Dr. Hank), Adam Grant, Chris Voss, Andy Cunningham, Drew Brannon, Lorenzo Diaz-Mataix, and Julia Kristina all generously took time to share their knowledge, wisdom, and experiences through personal conversations and interviews. Along with them, Brian Brandt,

Trent Selbrede, and Kristin Sherry helped me refine and clarify my own ideas.

Kevin Kruse and Sally Hogshead generously shared writing and publishing gold with me.

The entire team at Page Two was invaluable in helping me write and produce this book. Jesse Finkelstein gave me an amazing gift—the vision for what this book could be (and should be). Gabi Narsted went above and beyond in coordinating the team's efforts and keeping us on schedule. My editor, Amanda Lewis, was everything I hoped for; she helped me hone the book's strengths, greatly improve its weaknesses, and see my words through the eyes of the reader—while cheering me on along the way. May Antaki and Jenny Govier helped me further refine and clarify—so the words on the page truly represented the words in my head.

Peter Cocking, Taysia Louie, and Aksara Mantra contributed to the book's beautiful design, both inside and outside. And thankfully so, since we all know people *do* judge a book by its cover... and by the way it looks on the inside, too.

Ivette K. Caballero's unique combination of smarts, experience, and hustle made her the perfect choice to lead the book's marketing effort. Michelle Alwine is a brilliant communicator, and a pleasure to work with. Together, they got this book into the hands of more readers than I ever could have on my own.

Special thanks also to LeRon Pinder, Ruth Flores, Francis Bonilla, Myron Loggins, Chris and Sugeiri Brown, Masai Collins, Joe and April Paglia, Craig Martin, Dan and Priscilla Pecsok, Skip and Geege Koehler, Ralph and Sasha Mejia, Ernie and Diana Reed, Chris Boyce, Sherman Butts, Kevin Clanton, David and Arnie Locquiao, Curtis and Marlene Walters, Quirin and Jemima Gumadlas, the Marcelo family, the Peña family, the Porcema family, the Jose family, Stefan and

Cherry Sanidad, Phil and Irish Santiago, Kevin and Mayleen
Smith, Ronnel Tuazon, Chelsea and Joshua Pulcifer, Tim and
Monica Purscell, James Flood, Pete and Rebecca Schmeichel,
Jim and Christa Birner, Jogesh Khana, Eric and Loida Lundy,
Derrel Jones, Giraud Jackson, Jeremy and Zuleka Murrie,
Eddie Castillo, Lena Johnson, Franklin and Rita Saucedo,
Michael and Rebecca Gietler, Phil and Michelle Geringer,
Gerry and Amy Navarro, Tim and Pam Zalesky, Joe Lueken,
Aquil Khan, Glenn Balmes, Connie and Jonathan Lei, Genelle
Morrison, Johnathan and Maureen Dimalanta, Melvin
Dimalanta, Erick and Erica Calunsag, Rodge Jansuy, Mitch
and Bridgeta Lipayon, Eric Islas, Randy and Johanna Rosabal,
Omar Morales, Noe Luna, Joe and Barbara Lynch, Patrick and
Rachel Swann, Mark and Linda Sprankle, the Vadala family,
Don and Andria Benjamin, the Rivera family, Spencer and
Rachel Wetten, Micah and Ashlie Helie, the Boie family, Anne
Brackett, Sia Stephanos, Sally Thornton, Mike and Jennifer
Reis, Dawn and Todd Meyer, Zoe and Bill Conger, the Ward-
low family, Gary and Linda Gorum, the Robertson family, the
Campau family, the Lello family, Michael and Theresa O'Neill,
Isabel and Ray Perez, the Mattson family, Jocelyn and Darius
Whitten, Beverly Stephens, Lemar and Rabiha Garnett, the
Al-Shaffi family, Matthias and Avelina Eichler, Ben and Monika
Jenkins, Manuel and Hana Krause, Stefan Steiner, Jeremy
Borkovic, Hannelore and Peter Mitrega, Harald and Sybille
Beinczyk, Pieter and Karen Vousden, Rainald and Ruth Kahle,
Niki and Nikita Karlstroem, Daniel and Dolores Hahn, Solano
and Cyndi Williams, Virgil and Deidre Card, Dan and Katie
Houghton, Alex and Tabitha Scholz, the Quohilag family,
Fernand and Jill Oundjian, Olga and Adam Grzelczyk, Magda
and Rafal Szjabel, Lidia Mikunda, Agnieszka Zachariasz, Nella
and Olli Schueller, Ernst and Jessica Schneidereit, Russ and
Arianne Miller, Tim Kouloumpas, Michael Reinmueller, Alex

Reinmueller, Mark Noumair, Guy Pierce, Gerritt Lösch, Bobby and Galina Rivera, Kris and Doro Sistrunk, Falko and Dani Burkmann, Moritz and Vroni Strauss, Loren and Elsbeth Klawa, the Zachariadis family, the Ohene-Korang family, the Ordonez family, Bernd and Inge Wrobel, Silas and Melanie Burgfeld, the Schwicker family, the Ouedraogo family, the Schoemer family, Vasilis and Veronika Chantzaras, Sonja and Uwe Herrmann, Elsbeth and Lorén Klawa, the Latimer family, Daniel and Rachel Pilley, the Rosenzweig family, Nora Smith, Virginia and Anais Chan, Daniel Wirthmueller, Jack and Caroline Simpson, Albin Fritz, Bill and Jason Liber, Sebastian Elstner, the Rurainski family, and many others who I will regret not naming here. I have learned so much from all of them.

My children, Jonah and Lily, have inspired emotions on a level different than anything I have ever experienced. I see so much of myself in Jonah that I can't believe my eyes and ears. Lily is full of surprises, and all the emotional intelligence in the world can't protect me from her charm. (I hope she chooses to use it for good and not for evil.) Every day, my heart swells with pride for these two and I thank Jehovah that he's blessed me with the pleasure, responsibility, and privilege of raising them.

And finally, there's my wife, Dominika. I knew you were special from the moment we met, and you've continued to impress me ever since. Ten years married, and I'm more deeply in love with you than ever. You help me to be the best version of myself. You are my everything. Without you, I'm lost—literally.

But with you, I'm the happiest man on earth.

References

Chapter 1: From Theory to Practice

6   "I spent five years working closely with Steve": Andy Cunningham, interview by author, December 8, 2017.

7   *Emotional Intelligence* would spend: "About Daniel Goleman," Daniel Goleman (website), accessed January 7, 2018, www.danielgoleman.info/biography.

7   Howard Gardner theorized: Howard Gardner, *Frames of Mind: The Theory of Multiple Intelligences*, 3rd ed. (New York: Basic Books, 2011).

8   Mayer and Salovey described it this way: Peter Salovey and John D. Mayer, "Emotional Intelligence," *Imagination, Cognition, and Personality* 9, no. 3 (1990): 185-211, http://ei.yale.edu/wp-content/uploads/2014/06/pub153_SaloveyMayerICP1990_OCR.pdf.

9   Footnote: Daniel Goleman, Richard Boyatzis, and Annie McKee, *Primal Leadership: Unleashing the Power of Emotional Intelligence* (Boston: Harvard Business Review Press, 2013).

12   Footnote: Carol S. Dweck, *Mindset: The New Psychology of Success* (New York: Random House, 2006).

14   When his biographer Walter Isaacson asked him: Walter Isaacson, *Steve Jobs* (New York: Simon & Schuster, 2011).

Chapter 2: Under Control

17   "As the birds hit the plane": Chesley B. "Sully" Sullenberger III and Jeffrey Zaslow, *Sully: My Search for What Really Matters* (New York: William Morrow, 2016).

19   "I think in many ways, as it turned out": Chesley Sullenberger, interview by Katie Couric, *60 Minutes*, CBS, February 8, 2009.

28   "We're scared of the big, amorphous blob": Andrea Bonoir, "The Surefire First Step to Stop Procrastinating," *Psychology Today*, May 1, 2014, www.psychologytoday.com/blog/friendship-20/201405/the-surefire-first-step-stop-procrastinating.

31   Research indicates that lack of proper sleep: Louise Beattie, Simon D. Kyle, Colin A. Espie, and Stephany M. Biello, "Social Interactions, Emotion and Sleep: A Systematic Review and Research Agenda," *Sleep Medicine Reviews* 24 (2015): 83-100.

31   "'Negative' moods summon a more attentive": Susan David, *Emotional Agility: Get Unstuck, Embrace Change, and Thrive in Work and Life* (New York: Penguin, 2016).

32   explains one way you can do this: Lisa Feldman Barrett, *How Emotions Are Made: The Secret Life of the Brain* (New York: Houghton Mifflin Harcourt, 2017).

32   For example, students who were taking: Jeremy P. Jamieson, Wendy Berry Mendes, Erin Blackstock, and Toni Schmader, "Turning the Knots in Your Stomach into Bows: Reappraising Arousal Improves Performance on the GRE," *Journal of Experimental Social Psychology* 46, no. 1 (2010): 208-212.

32   The "excited" participants: Alison Wood Brooks, "Get Excited: Reappraising Pre-performance Anxiety as Excitement," *Journal of Experimental Psychology: General* 143, no. 3 (2013): 1144-1158.

34   Recent studies suggest that reading fiction: David Kidd and Emanuele Castano, "Different Stories: How Levels of Familiarity with Literary and Genre Fiction Relate to Mentalizing," *Psychology of Aesthetics, Creativity, and the Arts* 11, no. 4 (2017): 474-486; P. Matthijs Bal and Martijn Veltkamp, "How Does Fiction Reading Influence Empathy? An Experimental Investigation on the Role of Emotional Transportation," *PLOS One* 8, no. 1 (2013): e55341.

35   In a systematic review of thirty-six studies: Beattie, "Social Interactions, Emotion and Sleep."

35   More and more research suggests that writing: Karen A. Baikie and Kay Wilhelm, "Emotional and Physical Health Benefits of Expressive Writing," *Advances in Psychiatric Treatment* 11, no. 5 (2005): 338-346.

35   extended travel can promote: Julia Zimmermann and Franz J. Neyer, "Do We Become a Different Person When Hitting the Road? Personality Development of Sojourners," *Journal of Personality and Social Psychology* 105, no. 3 (2013): 515.

35   "a hero is someone who risks his life": Sullenberger, *Sully.*

Chapter 3: Creatures of Habit

40   "For decades, neuroscientists assumed": Richard J. Davidson, *The Emotional Life of Your Brain: How Its Unique Patterns Affect the Way You Think, Feel, and Live—and How You Can Change Them* (New York: Penguin, 2012).

40   This philosophy harmonizes with the discoveries: Dweck, *Mindset.*

41   This reaction has to do with the amygdala: Joseph E. LeDoux, "Amygdala," *Scholarpedia* 3, no. 4 (2008): 2698.

46   "Habits, scientists say, emerge because the brain": Charles Duhigg, *The Power of Habit: Why We Do What We Do in Life and Business* (New York: Random House, 2012).

48   "Brain studies suggest that across their lifetimes": Brent J. Atkinson, "Supplementing Couples Therapy with Methods

for Reconditioning Emotional Habits," *Family Therapy Magazine* 10, no. 3 (2011): 28-32, www.thecouplesclinic.com/pdf/Supplementing_Couples_Therapy.pdf.

Chapter 4: Diamonds in the Rough

53   This explains why Pete Wells: Pete Wells, "At Thomas Keller's Per Se, Slips and Stumbles," *New York Times*, January 12, 2016.

54   "We pride ourselves": Thomas Keller, "To Our Guests," Thomas Keller Restaurant Group (website), accessed December 8, 2017, www.thomaskeller.com/messagetoourguests.

54   "Maybe we were complacent": Gabe Ulla, "Can Thomas Keller Turn Around Per Se?" *Town & Country*, October 2016.

56   "At Amazon, workers are encouraged": Jodi Kantor and David Streitfeld, "Inside Amazon: Wrestling Big Ideas in a Bruising Workplace," *New York Times*, August 16, 2015.

56   and even sparked a public debate: Dean Baquet, "Dean Baquet Responds to Jay Carney's *Medium* Post," *Medium*, October 19, 2015, https://medium.com/@NYTimesComm/dean-baquet-responds-to-jay-carney-s-medium-post-6af794c7a7c6.

57   Bezos even invited employees: John Cook, "Full Memo: Jeff Bezos Responds to Brutal NYT Story, Says It Doesn't Represent the Amazon He Leads," GeekWire, August 16, 2015, www.geekwire.com/2015/full-memo-jeff-bezos-responds-to-cutting-nyt-expose-says-tolerance-for-lack-of-empathy-needs-to-be-zero.

57   In an official statement, the new process: Taylor Soper, "Amazon to 'Radically' Simplify Employee Reviews, Changing Controversial Program amid Huge Growth," GeekWire, November 14, 2016, www.geekwire.com/2016/amazon-radically-simplify-employee-reviews-changing-controversial-program-amid-huge-growth.

61 "The most common form of manipulation": Mike Myatt, *Hacking Leadership: The 11 Gaps Every Business Needs to Close and the Secrets to Closing Them Quickly* (Hoboken, NJ: Wiley, 2013).

61 Footnote: Agence France-Presse, "Parents Who Praise Children Too Much May Encourage Narcissism, Says Study," *Guardian*, March 10, 2015, www.theguardian.com/world/2015/mar/10/parents-who-praise-children-too-much-may-encourage-narcissism-says-study.

64 "Someone who's asking for coaching": Sheila Heen and Douglas Stone, "Find the Coaching in Criticism," *Harvard Business Review*, January/February 2014, https://hbr.org/2014/01/find-the-coaching-in-criticism.

64 Footnote: Carolyn O'Hara, "How to Get the Feedback You Need," *Harvard Business Review*, May 15, 2015, https://hbr.org/2015/05/how-to-get-the-feedback-you-need.

66 "I would love to have received that criticism": Peter Holley, "He Was Minutes from Retirement," *Washington Post*, December 12, 2016, www.washingtonpost.com/news/on-leadership/wp/2016/12/12/he-was-minutes-from-retirement-but-first-he-blasted-his-bosses-in-a-company-wide-email.

Chapter 5: The Truth about Empathy

71 The English word "empathy": Susan Lanzoni, "A Short History of Empathy," *Atlantic*, October 15, 2015, www.theatlantic.com/health/archive/2015/10/a-short-history-of-empathy/409912.

72 break down the concept of empathy: Daniel Goleman, "Three Kinds of Empathy," Daniel Goleman (website), June 12, 2007, www.danielgoleman.info/three-kinds-of-empathy-cognitive-emotional-compassionate.

75 in which participants predicted how painful: Adam Grant, *Give and Take: Why Helping Others Drives Our Success* (New York: Penguin Books, 2014).

76   "When we are dealing with our vices": Shankar Vedantam, "Hot and Cold Emotions Make Us Poor Judges," *Washington Post,* August 6, 2007.

83   Bloom argues that empathy has the tendency: Paul Bloom, *Against Empathy: The Case for Rational Compassion* (New York: Ecco, 2016).

84   The temptation is for caregivers: Barbara Lombardo and Caryl Eyre. 2011, "Compassion Fatigue: A Nurse's Primer," *Online Journal of Issues in Nursing* 16, no. 1 (2011): 3; Maryann Abendroth and Jeanne Flannery, "Predicting the Risk of Compassion Fatigue," *Journal of Hospice and Palliative Nursing* 8, no. 6 (2006): 346-356.

85   Of course, you don't have to be a nurse: Robin Stern and Diane Divecha, "The Empathy Trap," *Psychology Today,* May 4, 2015, www.psychologytoday.com/articles/201505/the-empathy-trap.

85   in certain cases, the use of social media: Keith Hampton, Lee Rainie, Weixu Lu, Inyoung Shin, and Kristen Purcell, "Social Media and the Cost of Caring," Pew Research Center (website), January 15, 2015, www.pewinternet.org/2015/01/15/social-media-and-stress.

88   "I think when tragedy occurs": Sheryl Sandberg, "Today is the end of sheloshim for my beloved husband," Facebook, June 3, 2015, www.facebook.com/sheryl/posts/10155617891025177.

88   "I was grateful every day": Sheryl Sandberg, "There have been many times when I've been grateful to work at companies that supported families," Facebook, February 7, 2017, www.facebook.com/sheryl/posts/10158115250050177.

90   "Mr. Pierce served": "Guy H. Pierce, Member of the Governing Body of Jehovah's Witnesses, Dies," Jehovah's Witnesses (website), March 20, 2014, www.jw.org/en/news/releases/by-region/world/guy-pierce-governing-body-member-dies.

Chapter 6: The Power of Influence

91   Voss recalls one day in 1998: Chris Voss and Tahl Raz, *Never Split the Difference: Negotiating as If Your Life Depended on It* (New York: HarperBusiness, 2016).

92   "It's not me bringing emotion in": Chris Voss, interview by author, February 9, 2018.

95   the time he met a distinguished botanist: Dale Carnegie, *How to Win Friends & Influence People* (New York: Simon and Schuster, 1981).

99   "Effective persuaders must be adept": Jay Conger, *The Necessary Art of Persuasion* (Boston: Harvard Business Review Press, 2008).

104   For example, writer friend Lyz Lenz once penned: Lyz Lenz, "Dear Daughter, I Want You to Fail," Huffington Post, February 24, 2013, www.huffingtonpost.com/lyz-lenz/snow-plow-parents_b_2735929.html.

106   She was performing in front of a crowd: Ramona G. Almirez, "Celine Dion Reacts Calmly to Fan Storming Stage," Storyful Rights Management, January 8, 2018, https://youtu.be/GoO2LpfcVVI.

Chapter 7: Building Bridges

111   Footnote: Harvard Study of Adult Development (website), accessed January 13, 2018, www.adultdevelopmentstudy.org; Robert J. Waldinger, "What Makes a Good Life? Lessons from the Longest Study on Happiness," TED Talks, December 1, 2015, www.ted.com/talks/robert_waldinger_what_makes_a_good_life_lessons_from_the_longest_study_on_happiness.

111   The research team analyzed: Julia Rozovsky, "The Five Keys to a Successful Google Team," *re:Work* (blog), November 17, 2015, https://rework.withgoogle.com/blog/five-keys-to-a-successful-google-team.

113   the most effective managers: Jim Harter and Amy Adkins, "Employees Want a Lot More from Their Managers," Gallup Business Journal (website), April 8, 2015, http:// news.gallup.com/businessjournal/182321/employees-lot-managers.aspx.

114   Asked about the worst career advice: Angela Ahrendts, interview by Rebecca Jarvis, *No Limits with Rebecca Jarvis*, ABC Radio, January 9, 2018.

119   Researchers have found that promise-makers: Thomas Baumgartner, Urs Fischbacher, Anja Feierabend, Kai Lutz, and Ernst Fehr, "The Neural Circuitry of a Broken Promise," *Neuron* 64, no. 5 (2009): 756-770.

122   highlighted the value of praise: Dan Ariely, *Payoff: The Hidden Logic That Shapes Our Motivations* (New York: Simon & Schuster/TED, 2016).

123   "We're worried about the other person's reaction": Erika Andersen, "Why We Hate Giving Feedback—and How to Make It Easier," *Forbes,* January 12, 2012, www.forbes.com/ sites/erikaandersen/2012/06/20/why-we-hate-giving-feedback-and-how-to-make-it-easier.

127   "The company's stock was falling steeply": Rodger Dean Duncan, "How Campbell's Soup's Former CEO Turned the Company Around," *Fast Company,* September 18, 2014, www. fastcompany.com/3035830/how-campbells-soups-former-ceo-turned-the-company-around.

Chapter 8: The Dark Side

132   As Hitler's speeches began attracting: Nick Enoch, "Mein Camp: Unseen Pictures of Hitler... in a Very Tight Pair of Lederhosen," *Daily Mail,* July 3, 2014, www.dailymail.co.uk/ news/article-2098223/Pictures-Hitler-rehearsing-hate-filled-speeches.html.

132 "Disturbingly, many of Hitler's early measures": Alex Gendler and Anthony Hazard, "How Did Hitler Rise to Power?" TED-Ed, July 18, 2016, https://youtu.be/jFICRFKtAc4.

133 They describe Iago as: Ursa K.J. Naglera, Katharina J. Reiter, Marco R. Furtner, and John F. Rauthmann, "Is There a 'Dark Intelligence'? Emotional Intelligence Is Used by Dark Personalities to Emotionally Manipulate Others," *Personality and Individual Differences* 65 (2014): 47-52.

135 "Often they're our friends": Tom Chivers, "How to Spot a Psychopath," *Telegraph*, August 29, 2017, www.telegraph. co.uk/books/non-fiction/spot-psychopath.

135 "Taking charge, making decisions": Robert Hare and Paul Babiak, *Snakes in Suits: When Psychopaths Go to Work* (New York: HarperBusiness, 2007).

135 A group of German scientists found: Mitja D. Back, Stefan C. Schmukle, and Boris Egloff, "Why Are Narcissists So Charming at First Sight? Decoding the Narcissism–Popularity Link at Zero Acquaintance," *Journal of Personality and Social Psychology* 98, no. 1 (2010): 132-145.

135 A 2011 study indicated that "Machiavellians": Stéphane Côté, Katherine A. DeCelles, Julie M. McCarthy, Gerben A. Van Kleef, and Ivona Hideg, "The Jekyll and Hyde of Emotional Intelligence: Emotion-Regulation Knowledge Facilitates Both Prosocial and Interpersonally Deviant Behavior," *Psychological Science* 22, no. 8 (2011): 1073-1080.

136 A 2013 study found that those: Sara Konrath, Olivier Corneille, Brad J. Bushman, and Olivier Luminet, "The Relationship between Narcissistic Exploitativeness, Dispositional Empathy, and Emotion Recognition Abilities," *Journal of Nonverbal Behavior* 38, no. 1 (2014): 129-143.

136 "The root cause of sales practice failures": Independent Directors of the Board of Wells Fargo & Company Oversight Committee, *Sales Practices Investigation Report*, April 10, 2017.

137 "The sales pressure from management": Matt Egan, "Workers Tell Wells Fargo Horror Stories," CNN Money, September 9, 2016, http://money.cnn.com/2016/09/09/investing/wells-fargo-phony-accounts-culture/index.html.

137 "You were stuck": Chris Arnold, "Former Wells Fargo Employees Describe Toxic Sales Culture, Even at HQ," NPR, October 4, 2016, www.npr.org/2016/10/04/496508361/former-wells-fargo-employees-describe-toxic-sales-culture-even-at-hq.

138 While it's difficult to estimate: Jen Wieczner, "How Wells Fargo's Carrie Tolstedt Went from *Fortune* Most Powerful Woman to Villain," *Fortune*, April 10, 2017, http://fortune.com/2017/04/10/wells-fargo-carrie-tolstedt-clawback-net-worth-fortune-mpw.

138 In one study on emotional behavior: Joanne Martin, Kathleen Knopoff, and Christine Beckman, "An Alternative to Bureaucratic Impersonality and Emotional Labor: Bounded Emotionality at The Body Shop," *Administrative Science Quarterly* 43, no. 2 (1998): 429-469.

139 But as details of the experiment emerged: Robinson Meyer, "Everything We Know about Facebook's Secret Mood Manipulation Experiment," *Atlantic*, June 28, 2014, www.theatlantic.com/technology/archive/2014/06/everything-we-know-about-facebooks-secret-mood-manipulation-experiment/373648/#IRB.

140 "If someone is trying to get in our head": Drew Brannon, interview by author, January 21, 2018.

142 "Also be wary of organizations": "The Breaking News Consumer's Handbook," *On the Media Blog*, WNYC, September 20, 2013, www.wnyc.org/story/breaking-news-consumers-handbook-pdf.

143 "If a news organization says": "The Breaking News Consumer's Handbook," *On the Media Blog*.

143 Footnote: Olivia Solon, "The Future of Fake News: Don't Believe Everything You Read, See or Hear," *Guardian,* July 26, 2017, www.theguardian.com/technology/2017/jul/26/fake-news-obama-video-trump-face2face-doctored-content.

145 The problem is that some people use: Robert Cialdini, *Influence: The Psychology of Persuasion,* rev. ed. (New York: Harper Collins, 2009).

147 the only way to truly address passive-aggressiveness: Signe Whitson, "6 Tips for Confronting Passive-Aggressive People," *Psychology Today,* January 11, 2016, www.psychologytoday.com/blog/passive-aggressive-diaries/201601/6-tips-confronting-passive-aggressive-people.

148 "Love bombing is an attempt to influence": Dale Archer, "Why Love-Bombing a Relationship Is So Devious," *Psychology Today,* March 6, 2017, www.psychologytoday.com/blog/reading-between-the-headlines/201703/why-love-bombing-in-relationship-is-so-devious.

150 Multiple women claimed that Weinstein: Jodi Kantor and Megan Twohey, "Harvey Weinstein Paid Off Sexual Harassment Accusers for Decades," *New York Times,* October 5, 2017, www.nytimes.com/2017/10/05/us/harvey-weinstein-harassment-allegations.html.

150 Millions used the social media hashtag #MeToo: Cristela Guerra, "Where Did 'Me Too' Come From? Activist Tarana Burke, Long before Hashtags," *Boston Globe,* October 17, 2017, www.bostonglobe.com/lifestyle/2017/10/17/alyssa-milano-credits-activist-tarana-burke-with-founding-metoo-movement-years-ago/o2Jv29v6ljObkKPTPB9KGP/story.html.

151 "There's a monumental amount of work": Sophie Gilbert, "The Movement of #MeToo," *Atlantic,* October 16, 2017, www.theatlantic.com/entertainment/archive/2017/10/the-movement-of-metoo/542979.

Bibliography

Abendroth, Maryann, and Jeanne Flannery. "Predicting the Risk of Compassion Fatigue." *Journal of Hospice and Palliative Nursing* 8, no. 6 (2006): 346-356.

Agence France-Presse. "Parents Who Praise Children Too Much May Encourage Narcissism, Says Study." *Guardian*, March 10, 2015. www.theguardian.com/world/2015/mar/10/parents-who-praise-children-too-much-may-encourage-narcissism-says-study.

Ahrendts, Angela. "The Self-Proclaimed 'Non-Techie' Leading Apple Retail Strategy." Interview by Rebecca Jarvis. *No Limits with Rebecca Jarvis*. ABC Radio, January 9, 2018.

Almirez, Ramona G. "Celine Dion Reacts Calmly to Fan Storming Stage." Storyful Rights Management, January 8, 2018. https://www.youtube.com/Goo2Lpfcvvi.

American Academy of Achievement. "Thomas Keller." Accessed January 7, 2017. www.achievement.org/achiever/thomas-keller-2.

Andersen, Erika. "Why We Hate Giving Feedback—and How to Make It Easier." *Forbes*, January 12, 2012. www.forbes.com/sites/erikaandersen/2012/06/20/why-we-hate-giving-feedback-and-how-to-make-it-easier.

Archer, Dale. "Why Love-Bombing in a Relationship Is So Devious." *Psychology Today*, March 6, 2017. www. psychologytoday.com/blog/reading-between-the-headlines/201703/why-love-bombing-in-relationship-is-so-devious.

Ariely, Dan. *Payoff: The Hidden Logic That Shapes Our Motivations.* New York: Simon & Schuster/TED, 2016.

Arnold, Chris. "Former Wells Fargo Employees Describe Toxic Sales Culture, Even at HQ." NPR, October 4, 2016. www.npr.org/2016/10/04/496508361/former-wells-fargo-employees-describe-toxic-sales-culture-even-at-hq.

Atkinson, Brent J. "Supplementing Couples Therapy with Methods for Reconditioning Emotional Habits." *Family Therapy Magazine* 10, no. 3 (2011): 28-32. www.thecouplesclinic.com/pdf/Supplementing_Couples_Therapy.pdf.

Back, Mitja D., Stefan C. Schmukle, and Boris Egloff. "Why Are Narcissists So Charming at First Sight? Decoding the Narcissism–Popularity Link at Zero Acquaintance." *Journal of Personality and Social Psychology* 98, no. 1 (2010): 132-145.

Baikie, Karen A., and Kay Wilhelm. "Emotional and Physical Health Benefits of Expressive Writing." *Advances in Psychiatric Treatment* 11, no. 5 (2005): 338-346.

Bal, P. Matthijs, and Martijn Veltkamp. "How Does Fiction Reading Influence Empathy? An Experimental Investigation on the Role of Emotional Transportation." *PLOS One* 8, no. 1 (2013): e55341.

Baquet, Dean. "Dean Baquet Responds to Jay Carney's *Medium* Post." *Medium*, October 19, 2015. https://medium.com/@NyTimesComm/dean-baquet-responds-to-jay-carney-s-medium-post-6af794c7a7c6.

Barrett, Lisa Feldman. *How Emotions Are Made: The Secret Life of the Brain.* New York: Houghton Mifflin Harcourt, 2017.

Baumgartner, Thomas, Urs Fischbacher, Anja Feierabend, Kai Lutz, and Ernst Fehr. "The Neural Circuitry of a Broken Promise." *Neuron* 64, no. 5 (2009): 756-770.

Beattie, Louise, Simon D. Kyle, Colin A. Espie, and Stephany M. Biello. "Social Interactions, Emotion and Sleep: A Systematic Review and Research Agenda." *Sleep Medicine Reviews* 24 (2015): 83-100.

Bloom, Paul. *Against Empathy: The Case for Rational Compassion.* New York: Ecco, 2016.

Bonoir, Andrea. "The Surefire First Step to Stop Procrastinating." *Psychology Today*, May 1, 2014. www.psychologytoday.com/blog/friendship-20/201405/the-surefire-first-step-stop-procrastinating.

Brooks, Alison Wood. "Get Excited: Reappraising Pre-performance Anxiety as Excitement." *Journal of Experimental Psychology: General* 143, no. 3 (2013): 1144-1158.

Brooks, David. "The Golden Age of Bailing." *New York Times*, July 7, 2017. www.nytimes.com/2017/07/07/opinion/the-golden-age-of-bailing.html.

Bryant, Adam. "Corey E. Thomas of Rapid7 on Why Companies Succeed or Fail." *New York Times*, August 18, 2017. www.nytimes.com/2017/08/18/business/corner-office-corey-thomas-rapid7.html.

Carnegie, Dale. *How to Win Friends & Influence People.* New York: Simon and Schuster, 1981.

Carney, Jay. "What the *New York Times* Didn't Tell You." *Medium*, October 19, 2015. https://medium.com/@jaycarney/what-the-new-york-times-didn-t-tell-you-a1128aa78931.

Chivers, Tom. "How to Spot a Psychopath." *Telegraph*, August 29, 2017. www.telegraph.co.uk/books/non-fiction/spot-psychopath.

Cialdini, Robert. *Influence: The Psychology of Persuasion.* Rev. ed. New York: Harper Collins, 2009.

Conger, Jay. *The Necessary Art of Persuasion.* Boston: Harvard Business Review Press, 2008.

Cook, John. "Full Memo: Jeff Bezos Responds to Brutal NYT Story, Says It Doesn't Represent the Amazon He Leads." GeekWire,

August 16, 2015. www.geekwire.com/2015/full-memo-jeff-bezos-responds-to-cutting-nyt-expose-says-tolerance-for-lack-of-empathy-needs-to-be-zero.

Côté, Stéphane, Katherine A. DeCelles, Julie M. McCarthy, Gerben A. Van Kleef, and Ivona Hideg. "The Jekyll and Hyde of Emotional Intelligence: Emotion-Regulation Knowledge Facilitates Both Prosocial and Interpersonally Deviant Behavior." *Psychological Science* 22, no. 8 (2011): 1073-1080.

D'Alessandro, Carianne. "Dropbox's CEO Was Late to a Company-wide Meeting on Punctuality. What Followed Wasn't Pretty." Inc. com, July 6, 2017. www.inc.com/video/drew-houston/how-dropboxs-ceo-learned-an-embarrassing-lesson-on-leadership.html.

David, Susan. *Emotional Agility: Get Unstuck, Embrace Change, and Thrive in Work and Life*. New York: Penguin, 2016.

Davidson, Richard J. *The Emotional Life of Your Brain: How Its Unique Patterns Affect the Way You Think, Feel, and Live—and How You Can Change Them*. New York: Penguin, 2012.

Donne, John. *Devotions upon Emergent Occasions*. Edited by Anthony Raspa. Montreal: McGill-Queen's University Press, 1975.

Duhigg, Charles. *The Power of Habit: Why We Do What We Do in Life and Business*. New York: Random House, 2012.

Duncan, Rodger Dean. "How Campbell's Soup's Former CEO Turned the Company Around." *Fast Company*, September 18, 2014. www.fastcompany.com/3035830/how-campbells-soups-former-ceo-turned-the-company-around.

Durant, Will. *The Story of Philosophy: The Lives and Opinions of the World's Greatest Philosophers*. New York: Simon & Schuster, 1953.

Dweck, Carol S. *Mindset: The New Psychology of Success*. New York: Random House, 2006.

Egan, Danielle. "Into the Mind of a Psychopath." *Discover*, June 2016.

Egan, Matt. "Workers Tell Wells Fargo Horror Stories." CNN Money, September 9, 2016. http://money.cnn.com/2016/09/09/investing/wells-fargo-phony-accounts-culture/index.html.

Enoch, Nick. "Mein Camp: Unseen Pictures of Hitler... in a Very Tight Pair of Lederhosen." *Daily Mail*, July 3, 2014. www.dailymail.co.uk/news/article-2098223/Pictures-Hitler-rehearsing-hate-filled-speeches.html.

Friedman, Milton. *Capitalism and Freedom*. Fortieth anniversary ed. Chicago: University of Chicago Press, 2002.

Gardner, Howard. *Frames of Mind: The Theory of Multiple Intelligences*. 3rd ed. New York: Basic Books, 2011.

Gendler, Alex, and Anthony Hazard. "How Did Hitler Rise to Power?" TED-Ed, July 18, 2016. https://youtu.be/jFICRFKtAc4.

Gilbert, Elizabeth. *Eat, Pray, Love: One Woman's Search for Everything across Italy, India and Indonesia*. New York: Penguin, 2007.

Gilbert, Sophie. "The Movement of #MeToo." *Atlantic*, October 16, 2017. www.theatlantic.com/entertainment/archive/2017/10/the-movement-of-metoo/542979.

Goleman, Daniel. "About Daniel Goleman." Daniel Goleman (website). Accessed January 7, 2018. www.danielgoleman.info/biography.

———. "Three Kinds of Empathy." Daniel Goleman (website), June 12, 2007. www.danielgoleman.info/three-kinds-of-empathy-cognitive-emotional-compassionate.

Goleman, Daniel, Richard Boyatzis, and Annie McKee. *Primal Leadership: Unleashing the Power of Emotional Intelligence*. Boston: Harvard Business Review Press, 2013.

Grant, Adam. *Give and Take: Why Helping Others Drives Our Success*. New York: Penguin Books, 2014.

Guerra, Cristela. "Where Did 'Me Too' Come From? Activist Tarana Burke, Long before Hashtags." *Boston Globe*, October 17, 2017. www.bostonglobe.com/lifestyle/2017/10/17/alyssa-milano-credits-activist-tarana-burke-with-founding-metoo-movement-years-ago/02Jv29v6ljObkKpTpB9Kgp/story.html.

Hampton, Keith, Lee Rainie, Weixu Lu, Inyoung Shin, and Kristen Purcell. "Social Media and the Cost of Caring." Pew

Research Center (website), January 15, 2015. www.pewinternet. org/2015/01/15/social-media-and-stress.

Hare, Robert, and Paul Babiak. *Snakes in Suits: When Psychopaths Go to Work.* New York: HarperBusiness, 2007.

Harter, Jim, and Amy Adkins. "Employees Want a Lot More from Their Managers." Gallup Business Journal (website), April 8, 2015. http://news.gallup.com/businessjournal/182321/employ-ees-lot-managers.aspx.

Harvard Medical School. Harvard Study of Adult Development (website). Accessed January 13, 2018. www.adultdevelopment-study.org.

Heen, Sheila, and Douglas Stone. "Find the Coaching in Criticism." *Harvard Business Review*, January/February 2014. https://hbr. org/2014/01/find-the-coaching-in-criticism.

Holley, Peter. "He Was Minutes from Retirement. But First, He Blasted His Bosses in a Company-Wide Email." *Washington Post*, December 12, 2016. www.washingtonpost.com/news/ on-leadership/wp/2016/12/12/he-was-minutes-from-retire-ment-but-first-he-blasted-his-bosses-in-a-company-wide-email.

Independent Directors of the Board of Wells Fargo & Company Oversight Committee. *Sales Practices Investigation Report.* Inde-pendent Directors of the Board of Wells Fargo & Company, April 10, 2017.

Isaacson, Walter. *Steve Jobs.* New York: Simon & Schuster, 2011.

Jamieson, Jeremy P., Wendy Berry Mendes, Erin Blackstock, and Toni Schmader. "Turning the Knots in Your Stomach into Bows: Reappraising Arousal Improves Performance on the GRE." *Journal of Experimental Social Psychology* 46, no. 1 (2010): 208-212.

Kantor, Jodi, and David Streitfeld. "Inside Amazon: Wrestling Big Ideas in a Bruising Workplace." *New York Times*, August 16, 2015.

Kantor, Jodi, and Megan Twohey. "Harvey Weinstein Paid Off Sex-ual Harassment Accusers for Decades." *New York Times*, October

5, 2017. www.nytimes.com/2017/10/05/us/harvey-weinstein-harassment-allegations.html.

Keller, Thomas. "To Our Guests." Thomas Keller Restaurant Group (website). Accessed December 8, 2017. www.thomaskeller.com/messagetoourguests.

Kidd, David, and Emanuele Castano. "Different Stories: How Levels of Familiarity with Literary and Genre Fiction Relate to Mentalizing." *Psychology of Aesthetics, Creativity, and the Arts* 11, no. 4 (2017): 474-486.

Konrath, Sara, Olivier Corneille, Brad J. Bushman, and Olivier Luminet. "The Relationship between Narcissistic Exploitativeness, Dispositional Empathy, and Emotion Recognition Abilities." *Journal of Nonverbal Behavior* 38, no. 1 (2014): 129-143.

Laborde, S., F. Dosseville, and M.S. Allen. "Emotional Intelligence in Sport and Exercise: A Systematic Review." *Scandinavian Journal of Medicine & Science in Sports* 26, no. 8 (2016): 862-874.

Lanzoni, Susan. "A Short History of Empathy." *Atlantic*, October 15, 2015. www.theatlantic.com/health/archive/2015/10/a-short-history-of-empathy/409912.

LeDoux, Joseph E. "Amygdala." *Scholarpedia* 3, no. 4 (2008): 2698. www.scholarpedia.org/article/Amygdala.

Lenz, Lyz. "Dear Daughter, I Want You to Fail." Huffington Post, February 24, 2013. www.huffingtonpost.com/lyz-lenz/snowplow-parents_b_2735929.html.

Lombardo, Barbara, and Caryl Eyre. "Compassion Fatigue: A Nurse's Primer." *Online Journal of Issues in Nursing* 16, no. 1 (2011): 3.

Martin, Joanne, Kathleen Knopoff, and Christine Beckman. "An Alternative to Bureaucratic Impersonality and Emotional Labor: Bounded Emotionality at The Body Shop." *Administrative Science Quarterly* 43, no. 2 (1998): 429-469.

Meyer, Robinson. "Everything We Know about Facebook's Secret Mood Manipulation Experiment." *Atlantic*, June 28, 2014. www.

theatlantic.com/technology/archive/2014/06/everything-we-know-about-facebooks-secret-mood-manipulation-experiment/373648/#iRB.

Moon, Shinji. *The Anatomy of Being*. Self-published, Lulu, 2013.

Myatt, Mike. *Hacking Leadership: The 11 Gaps Every Business Needs to Close and the Secrets to Closing Them Quickly*. Hoboken, NJ: Wiley, 2013.

Naglera, Ursa K.J., Katharina J. Reitera, Marco R. Furtnera, and John F. Rauthmann. "Is There a 'Dark Intelligence'? Emotional Intelligence Is Used by Dark Personalities to Emotionally Manipulate Others." *Personality and Individual Differences* 65 (2014): 47-52.

O'Hara, Carolyn. "How to Get the Feedback You Need." *Harvard Business Review*, May 15, 2015. https://hbr.org/2015/05/how-to-get-the-feedback-you-need.

On the Media Blog. "The Breaking News Consumer's Handbook." WNYC, September 20, 2013. www.wnyc.org/story/breaking-news-consumers-handbook-pdf.

Outlaw, Frank. Quoted in "What They're Saying." *San Antonio Light*, May 18, 1977, 7-B.

Rozovsky, Julia. "The Five Keys to a Successful Google Team," *re:Work* (blog), November 17, 2015. https://rework. withgoogle.com/blog/five-keys-to-a-successful-google-team.

Salovey, Peter, and John D. Mayer. "Emotional Intelligence." *Imagination, Cognition, and Personality* 9, no. 3 (1990): 185-211. http://ei.yale.edu/wp-content/uploads/2014/06/pub153_SaloveyMayeriCp1990_OCR.pdf.

Sandberg, Sheryl. "There have been many times when I've been grateful to work at companies that supported families." Facebook, February 7, 2017. www.facebook.com/sheryl/posts/10158115250050177.

―――. "Today is the end of sheloshim for my beloved husband." Facebook, June 3, 2015. www.facebook.com/sheryl/posts/10155617891025177.

Shakespeare, William. *Timon of Athens*. Edited by John Dover Wilson. Cambridge: Cambridge University Press, 1961.

Solon, Olivia. "The Future of Fake News: Don't Believe Everything You Read, See or Hear." *Guardian*, July 26, 2017. www.theguardian.com/technology/2017/jul/26/fake-news-obama-video-trump-face2face-doctored-content.

Soper, Taylor. "Amazon to 'Radically' Simplify Employee Reviews, Changing Controversial Program Amid Huge Growth." Geek Wire, November 14, 2016. www.geekwire.com/2016/amazon-radically-simplify-employee-reviews-changing-controversial-program-amid-huge-growth.

Stern, Robin, and Diane Divecha. "The Empathy Trap." *Psychology Today*, May 4, 2015. www.psychologytoday.com/articles/201505/the-empathy-trap.

Sullenberger, Chesley. "I Was Sure I Could Do It." Interview by Katie Couric. *60 Minutes*. CBS, February 8, 2009.

Sullenberger, Chesley, and Jeffrey Zaslow. *Sully: My Search for What Really Matters*. New York: William Morrow, 2016.

Ulla, Gabe. "Can Thomas Keller Turn Around Per Se?" *Town & Country*, October 2016.

Vedantam, Shankar. "Hot and Cold Emotions Make Us Poor Judges." *Washington Post*, August 6, 2007.

Voss, Chris, and Tahl Raz. *Never Split the Difference: Negotiating As If Your Life Depended On It*. New York: HarperBusiness, 2016.

Waldinger, Robert J. "What Makes a Good Life? Lessons from the Longest Study on Happiness." TED Talks, December 1, 2015. www.ted.com/talks/robert_waldinger_what_makes_a_good_life_lessons_from_the_longest_ study_on_happiness.

Watch Tower Bible and Tract Society of Pennsylvania. "Guy H. Pierce, Member of the Governing Body of Jehovah's Witnesses, Dies." Jehovah's Witnesses (website), March 20, 2014. www.jw.org/en/news/releases/by-region/world/guy-pierce-governing-body-member-dies.

Wells, Pete. "At Thomas Keller's Per Se, Slips and Stumbles." *New York Times*, January 12, 2016.

Whitson, Signe. "6 Tips for Confronting Passive-Aggressive People." *Psychology Today*, January 11, 2016. www.psychologytoday. com/blog/passive-aggressive-diaries/201601/6-tips-confronting-passive-aggressive-people.

Wieczner, Jen. "How Wells Fargo's Carrie Tolstedt Went from *Fortune* Most Powerful Woman to Villain." *Fortune*, April 10, 2017. http://fortune.com/2017/04/10/wells-fargo-carrie-tolstedt-clawback-net-worth-fortune-mpw.

Wilde, Oscar. *The Soul of Man under Socialism*. London: Arthur L. Humphreys, 1900. Project Gutenberg ebook.

Zak, Paul. "The Neuroscience of Trust." *Harvard Business Review*, January/February 2017. https://hbr.org/2017/01/the-neuroscience-of-trust.

Zimmermann, Julia, and Franz J. Neyer. "Do We Become a Different Person When Hitting the Road? Personality Development of Sojourners." *Journal of Personality and Social Psychology* 105, no. 3 (2013): 515.

About the Author

JUSTIN BARISO IS an author, speaker, and consultant, and one of Inc.com's most popular columnists. His thoughts on leadership, management, and emotional intelligence have been featured by *TIME*, CNBC, and *Forbes*, among others. He has been recognized repeatedly by LinkedIn as a "Top Voice" in management and workplace culture.

Raised in a multicultural environment, Justin learned to see the world through different sets of eyes. He was fascinated by the way a single news report could inspire very different emotional reactions in others, based on factors like their age, background, and upbringing. After spending a decade in management for a major nonprofit, he moved to Europe and began his own consulting agency, where he has worked with a wide range of companies, from small businesses to Fortune 500 companies.

Today, Justin focuses on helping others harness the power of emotion for good.

Contact and Speaking

I'M EAGER TO share the research, interviews, and insights gathered over the years of writing this book. In practical terms, and using real-world examples, I highlight how emotional intelligence can be applied to everyday situations at work (and at home), and why doing so is more important than ever.

If you'd like to invite me to speak at your next event, reach out through LinkedIn or email at **info@eqapplied.com.**

Additionally, if this book has inspired insights or "aha" moments in your life, I'd love to hear them. If you disagree with my thoughts or would like to share constructive criticism, I'd love to hear that, too.

I look forward to hearing—and learning—from you.

Made in the USA
Las Vegas, NV
08 February 2022